W9-AOY-755

PROBLEMS OF THE CHURCH TODAY

Reprint of a series of twelve articles by eminent Theologians and churchmen originally appearing in L'Osservatore Romano.

BT 10 .U5

166497

1976

Publications Office

UNITED STATES CATHOLIC CONFERENCE

1312 Massachusetts Avenue, N.W.

Washington, D.C. 20005

Reprinted with permission

PREFACE

From December 1974 to March 1975 the English language weekly edition of *L'Osservatore Romano* published a series of twelve articles on doctrinal and practical problems of great importance for the life of the Church today.

These contributions, by highly qualified authors, give the reader wise and sure guidance on many important questions which are being widely debated today.

We are pleased therefore to be able to reproduce these articles in the present volume, by kind permission of *L'Osservatore Romano.* In this way they will obtain the wider readership which they deserve, and the study of them will be made easier and more fruitful for the reader.

CONTENTS

SACRED DOCTRINE IN THE CONTEMPORARY PASTORAL MINISTRY

by Rev. Barnabas Mary Ahern, C.P.

MEMBER OF THE THEOLOGICAL COMMISSION
PROFESSOR OF SACRED SCRIPTURE
AT THE PONTIFICAL GREGORIAN UNIVERSITY

Today, ten years after the close of Vatican Council II, we are able to see how effectively the Holy Spirit guided the Council Fathers in charting the course of authentic renewal in the Church. The years immediately following the Council often brought lowering clouds of confusion, faulty emphases, and misunderstanding. But happily this miasma is gradually disappearing, and a healthy atmosphere of light, order and peace is awakening new life in the Body of Christ.

This renewal of the Church derives primarily from the living word of God which the Holy Spirit has illumined and made efficacious. As at Thessalonica long ago, the perennial Gospel of Christ has come to the Church of today "not in mere words, but with the power of the Holy Spirit which makes for strong convictions" (1 Thess 1, 5). Fidelity to this Gospel is the best response the Spouse of Christ can offer to the ineffable mercy of God's total self-giving. For it is the triune God Himself who draws men to newness of life. As St. Paul affirms, the Father is the source of all redemptive and unifying love; Jesus the Son, God's perfect gift, expresses this love with the full willingness of His human heart; and the Holy Spirit, fire and unction, communicates God's gift of Himself to every person who will receive Him (cf. Rom. 5, 5-10; 2 Cor. 13, 13).

This saving action of the Trinity and the new, vital response to it in the life of the Church point up the opportunities and exigencies of the pastoral ministry. The renewal that is in course gives to the pastoral office a new stimulus and challenges it with urgent demand. Amid all its divergent activities and multifaceted modes of service, the ministry of the Church, if it is to have real impact upon the world, must work with renewed conviction that only "the Gospel of Christ is God's power to save those who believe" (Rom 1, 17). Apostles may use various means to plant and to water; but only God who reveals Himself and acts powerfully through the Gospel can "make things grow" (1 Cor 3, 7). In the light of this truth St. Augustine affirms that "saving faith is begotten, nourished, protected and strengthened" only by the sacred doctrine of God's word (*De Trin*. xiv, 1).

Therefore, to fulfill his mission of building up the Church, the apostolic workman faces a threefold task. First, he himself must be totally devoted to God's word; secondly, he must be a trustworthy ambassador in speaking this word; thirdly, he must recognize in God's word the only true bond of charity and unity in the Church. These three aspects of Gospel service have always inhered in the very nature of the pastoral ministry. Today, however, they have special resonances in a Church renewed by Vatican Council II.

1. The Minister's Love of Sacred Doctrine

"If the minister is to profess God's word to people, to nourish and strengthen their faith, he himself must grow in the understanding of revelation and in loving fidelity to the precepts of life which it offers."

The Gospel word is a "seed" that has more power than an atom bomb. Whereas the bomb can deal only death and destruction, the word of the Lord gives "spirit and life" (Jn 6, 63). When this seed falls into the good earth of a heart alive with faith it sinks roots and grows into fruitfulness. But there is nothing automatic in this growth. The word of God is not a magic abracadabra that transforms man apart from his own personal response. Rather, the revealed word manifesting the thoughts and will of God confronts its hearer as a person endowed with mind and will. As an intelligent person, therefore, the believer must consciously assimilate God's thoughts with grateful love and form in himself corresponding convictions. This sincere and alert faith begins a process of constant development. Because God's thoughts are as high above merely human thought as the heavens above the earth (Is 55, 9), the word which brings these thoughts of God to man in an ever-fruitful source of growing conformity to the Word Incarnate who is the perfect image of the Father's thought and will.

The Church herself has lived through this process of growth. While tenaciously faithful to the words of revelation, the Spouse of Christ, urged on by her great love of God, has gained luminous insights into the deep mysteries of revelation and its necessary consequences in human life. To paraphrase the words of Vincent of Lerins, "While dogma and conviction have remained always the same, there has been true growth in the Church's understanding and application of the divine word" (*Commonitorium,* 28; *MPL* 50, 668). This fact of the Church's development of the revealed word into sacred doctrine accounts for the fluidity of expression in the Question with which St. Thomas introduces his *Summa Theologica*. Reading this introduction one finds it difficult at times to determine whether the Angelic Doctor is speaking directly of the revealed word itself or of the sacred doctrine which authentically educes the rich wisdom inherent in God's word.

In an analogus way the minister of the Church must share the process of development in his own personal life. If he is to profess God's word to people to nourish and strengthen their faith, he himself must constantly grow in experiential understanding of revelation and in loving fidelity to the precepts of life which it offers. Like Paul the Apostle a true apostle should be able to boast, "If you read (or hear) my words, you will have some idea of the depths that I see in the mystery of Christ" (Eph 3, 4).

This personal development calls for both intellectual study and reflective prayerful pondering. In one of the most beautiful articles of the *Summa Theologica* (Pars. I, Q. 43, art. 5), St. Thomas explains that true Christian wisdom is not a barren speculative knowledge but an experiential understanding that is alive with love ("scientia cum amore"—ad 2). Looking to the mystery of the Divine Word in the Trinity, the Angelic Doctor observes that He is "not any sort of word, but the Word who breathes forth love" (ad 2). Hence He is the model of living faith. As the Divine Word cannot be thought of without the Holy Spirit who is love, so true Christian knowledge of the mysteries of God not only illumines the mind but also enkindles the affections (ad 3).

This ideal of personal growth in understanding the word of God is not a mirage. Vatican Council I insisted on the reality of this development: "When reason, illumined by faith, seeks earnestly, devoutly and reverently, it will attain by God's help a most fruitful understanding of the mysteries of God" (*Constitutio de fide catholica,* c. 4; *Denzinger-Rahner*, 1796). Fully aware that this personal growth was not only possible but imperative for the minister of the Gospel, St. Paul repeatedly urged his disciple Timothy to be the "good servant of Christ Jesus" who has "really digested the teaching of the faith and the good doctrine" (1 Tim 4, 6).

The need apostles have always had for an "absorbing interest" in God's word (cf. 1 Tim 4, 15) is especially urgent today when a pastor must often deal with people who are very well instructed and spiritually alive. As St Paul himself recognized, there is a reciprocity between the work of a pastor and the response of his flock (cf. Rom 1, 11-12). This interaction of mutual sharing and stimulation was emphasized in the 1971 Synodal document on the Ministerial Priesthood: "In the exercise of his ministry the priest is enlightened and strengthened by the action of the Church and the example of the faithful" (Part 2, I, 3). The role which the laity are now joyously undertaking in the liturgy, the interest in the Bible which they manifest in their study-clubs and biblical weeks, the resurgence of the life of prayer which has brought priest and people together for shared prayer and for group reflection on God's word—all of this requires the pastoral minister to be like Nepotian, St. Jerome's disciple, who "made his heart a living library of God's word." If an apostle is to fulfill his primary task of ministering the word of God to men, he must be "fully equipped and made ready" by personal devotedness to the word of God which makes him a humble and competent master of sacred doctrine (cf. 2 Tim 3, 16-17).

In the past few years this need has been widely recognized and provided for. Many dioceses have created centers, institutes, and symposia that priests may receive an ongoing education in the sacred sciences. This sound intellectual knowledge is of prime importance for the authenticity of Gospel ministry. Today, however, merely intellectual knowledge is not enough. Because our laity have come alive with a new love for the word of God that lives in scripture, liturgy, theology and the apostolate of justice and charity, the voice of the priest who mingles with them and speaks to them must ring with the accent of his own personal love for God's word. To achieve this authenticity a man must live the dictum of St. Thomas, "The will and the intellect mutually include each other" (*Summa Theol.* Pars. I, Q. 16, art. 4, ad 1). But this wondrous unity, essential for experiential knowledge of God's word is forged only in the fire of prayerful reflection wherein the Holy Spirit both illumines the mind and shapes the will.

Inaugurating a house of prayer for priests at Immaculate Conception Seminary, Huntington, N.Y., Bishop Kellenburg emphasized this serious need for studying the word of God with mind and heart. He said, "Because our priestly involvement with the faith is obvious, we cannot go for long periods without considering these fundamental questions: How deep is my personal relationship with God? How serious is my own commitment to prayer? To what degree am I able to face the Lord in the quiet of my own soul to share with Him my work, my needs, my goals and ideals?"

These pointed questions bear out a fundamental truth which St. Thomas emphasizes when he speaks of the nature of sacred doctrine. He insists that God is always its proper object. (Pars I, Q. 1, art. 7). Because all faith is simply man's loving response to God who reveals Himself and manifests His ways with men, the doctrine which develops this faith must itself look primarily to God. It is only in His light that man can see everything else as coming from Him and, if rightly used, leading to Him. Sacred doctrine, therefore, grows authentically through human understanding only if, like the apostles of the early Church, the minister of the Gospel unveils his heart in prayerful pondering to "reflect like a mirror the brightness of the Lord" that he may "radiate the light of the knowledge of God's glory, the glory shining on the face of Christ" (2 Cor 3, 18; 4, 6).

2. The Minister's Responsibility for Sacred Doctrine

"This forthright affirmation of Christian truth in the face of error is the urgent duty of every minister of the Gospel at the present time. As a teacher of faith, he is a man who stands responsible for the integrity of doctrine in the hearts of the faithful."

Devotion to the word of God can never be a merely personal factor in the life of the minister. Because, through God's call, he has been chosen to serve the Church and because, through ordination, he has been divinely empowered for this task, he bears grave responsibility to safeguard and promote the revelation of God in all its integrity. As God's appointed spokesman he must never belie, distort, or water down the contents of the divine message. This obligation, as negating all infidelity, binds him *semper et pro semper.*

The need to safeguard God's word has always been an essential duty of God's people. The Torah of Israel, summed up in the daily profession of faith—the *Shema'* (Deut 6, 4-9; 11, 13-21; Num 15, 37-41), emphasizes the need of God's people to hear (*Shama'*), to guard (*Shamar*), and to do (*'asah*) the words of God. This obligation carried special weight as the prime duty of the teachers of Israel, prophet and priest. Thus the Isaian Servant of Jahweh, the model of all prophetism, speaks of his need to be integrally faithful to God's word: "The Lord God has given me the tongue of a teacher. He sharpened my hearing that I might listen like one who is taught. The Lord God opened my ears and I did not disobey or turn back in defiance" (Is 50, 4-5).

Jesus, the perfect Servant of Jahweh, was unique in fulfilling this responsibility. Writing of Him, the "apostle and high priest of the religion we profess" (Heb 3, 1), the author of the Epistle to the Hebrews emphasizes Jesus' constant fidelity to the word and will of the Father. Using the single word "faithful," this epistle sums up the constant preoccupation of God's Son to echo perfectly in His teaching every word and promise of God: "The Son of God, Christ Jesus, was never a blend of Yes and No. With Him it was, and is, Yes. He is the Yes to every one of God's promises" (2 Cor 1, 19-20). Each time Jesus spoke of the word His Father revealed in the Torah He was so faithful to the meaning of that word that He cut away all false and superficial interpretations to declare the fullness of all that God intended (cf. Matt. 5, 17-48). Even when this authentic teaching aroused the hostility of the Scribes and Pharisees and, even though His fidelity to the Father's word would lead to His death, he held fixedly to the responsibility of His prophetic mission to deliver God's word without distortion or dilution: "Not a jot or tittle of the Law shall pass," He said, "until all things are accomplished" (Matt 5, 18).

Impelled by His own devotedness to the revealed word, Jesus insisted that the teachers of God's people in the New Covenant must be just as faithful as He was: "If any man sets aside even the least of the Law's demands, and teaches others to do the same, he will have the lowest place in the kingdom of heaven, whereas anyone who keeps the Law, and teaches others to do so, will stand high in the kingdom of heaven" (Matt. 5, 19).

It is little wonder, therefore, that Paul the Apostle, eminent teacher of the nations, echoes Jesus' insistence on the minister's obligation to preach the Gospel "without deceitfulness or any watering down the word of God . . . but by stating the truth openly in the sight of God" (2 Cor. 4, 2). The Apostle singles out responsibility and trustworthiness as the first duty of the minister who brings God's word to men (1 Cor. 4, 2). He warns that all preaching and teaching will be tested by the fire of an exacting judgment (1 Cor. 3, 11-15). Those who have been faithful to the Gospel will receive their reward; those who have distorted it will discover that their apostolic work has been useless.

St. Paul is very precise in explaining what this fidelity requires. Not content with vague and general allusions to the "Gospel," "the Word of God," "the foundation that is Christ Jesus," he reiterates frequently that the message which must be kept intact is authentically expressed in the sacred doctrine down in the catechetical teaching of the local churches; he calls this teaching *paradosis,* i.e., the integral message of Jesus transmitted by the Apostles and rightly interpreted in the Spirit-guided teaching of the Church. Twice the Apostle affirms that he himself had received from church teachers the instruction he needed on two essential points of faith, the Eucharist and the Resurrection of Jesus (1 Cor. 11, 23; 15, 3). Because this *paradosis* was taught to every convert and because it always included the same essentials (cf. Gal. 1, 6-9), St. Paul takes for granted that this universal and unchanging teaching is the patrimony of every local church. Hence, writing to the Colossians, a church which he had neither founded nor visited, Paul confidently urges his readers to be faithful to all they had learned from Epaphras, the founder of their church: "You must live your whole life according to the Christ you have received (in your catechetical instruction); you must be rooted in Him . . . and held fast by the faith you have received. Make sure that no one traps you by some second-hand, empty, rational philosophy based on the principles of this world instead of on Christ" (Col. 2, 6-8).

ILLUSORY RHETORIC

These words of St. Paul, interpreting faithfully the mind of Jesus, have been a beacon light in every age of the Church's life, preserving her from any falsification or distortion of the integral Gospel of Christ. Each time the doctrines of the Church have been threatened by the illusory rhetoric of man-made scientific or philosophic rationality, the pastors and theologians of the Church have been able to identify error by reason of its contrast with the unchanging word of God handed down in the sacred doctrine of the Church. This past year has seen two significant examples of this. An inter-demoninational group of concerned Christian scholars, meeting in Hartford, Connecticut, issued an "Appeal for Theological Affirmation" in which they repudiated thirteen pervasive themes that are "false and debilitating to the Church's life and work." At the same time, in Regensburg, Germany, twelve outstanding Catholic and Lutheran theologians called on contemporary Christianity to defend the full divinity of Christ against a heresy which has reduced Christ to a mere creature, the "man for others." In their strictures against error both of these groups of Christian scholars were simply reaffirming what the sacred doctrine of the Church has taught from the beginning.

OLD ERROR

This forthright affirmation of Christian truth in the face of error is the urgent duty of every minister of the Gospel at the present time. It would be naive to discount the inroads which Heideggerian Existentialist philosophy has made upon the faith of our people in the dogmatic and moral teaching of the revealed word. As applied to the interpretation of the New Testament by the Bultmannian school of Form-Criticism, the

Existentialist principles substitute mere words for the actual reality of the Christ-event which has saved the world. Everything supernatural in God's saving plan, i.e., the divine interventions in the virgin-birth of Jesus, in His miracles, in the redemptive power of His death and in the transformation of His real humanness through a corporeal resurrection —all this is seen as pure fabrication created by the early church to provide a God-inspired pattern for self-fulfillment. Only man-made words bind the "Christ of faith" to the "Jesus of history." Interpreted according to this false principle the New Testament reveals not an objective divine soteriology but only a so-called Christian anthropology devised by the genius of men.

It should be obvious to all that an old error has come back under a new label. Reductively, Bultmannism is but another form of Nominalism and Gnosticism. By ascribing man's salvation to mere faith in words and ideas this system belongs to the "worldly wisdom" which St. Paul condemned, because it "empties the cross of Christ of its efficacy as a divine event" (cf. 1 Cor. 1, 17).

The repercussions of this new nominalism on the moral teaching of the Church subjects the ethical imperatives of Christian life to the ebb and flow of sociological situation and psychological needs. In the same way this system would shape the contents and form of the sacramental life of the Church to accord with the constantly changing existential norm of contemporaneity. Instead of being a means of vital encounter with Christ in His "once for all" redemptive mystery, the sacraments and their liturgy would be volatilized into fluid symbols of the life and needs of the present Christian community.

To all this the Apostle Paul would respond with his fiery word of rejection, *"Me genoito!"* (Heaven forbid!). This expostulation which Paul uttered every time he saw a distortion of the *paradosis* must echo in the heart of every minister of the Church whenever he, too, confronts dogmatic error. As teacher of the faith, he is a man who stands responsible before God for the integrity of doctrine in the hearts of God's people. It must be his abiding conviction that when one truth of the faith is distorted or watered down, all truths of faith will suffer. Jesus Himself has taught that "even the least of God's words" must be treasured and safeguarded (Matt. 5, 19).

3. The Minister's Duty to promote Sacred Doctrine

"God's plan for our salvation is wondrous in its simplicity and unity. Every divine reality in Christian life comes from God's infinite love; and the purpose and power of each reality is to bear man to God."

At times a forthright condemnation of error is the only way a pastoral minister can safeguard the truth of the Gospel. However, most of our people are either unaware of false views propounded in scholarly circles or are frankly uninterested in the intricate reasoning that leads to and supports error. Unless something patently unchristian, like injustice or immorality, touches their daily life, they will not see the practical importance in their priest's censure of an error which seems to them esoteric and far removed. Practically, therefore, the best way for a minister to combat error is to present sacred doctrine in all its beauty, fullness and practicality.

The value of this positive presentation of truth is impressively evident in the letters of St. Paul. Though the Apostle bitterly condemned the errors which were weakening the faith in Galatia and Corinth, most often he strove to illumine his converts with a positive exposition of the full riches of the Christian message. Though a consummate theologian, Paul was, above all, a pastor. Hence, in dealing with his people, Paul consistently used sacred doctrine for the practical purpose of forming In them a truly Christian mind.

Thus he has little to say explicitly about the immanent life of the Trinity. Instead he sought to draw his Christians into this mystery by showing them how the Father, Son and Holy Spirit are always at work with divine power to realize in every human life their saving plan of love. To preserve his converts from the impurity which spoils Christian life Paul strengthened them with the reminder that the Holy Spirit was lovingly present and active in their very person; to sin would be an insult to this divine Spirit and a defilement of God's temple (cf. 1 Cor 6, 18-20; 1 Thess 4, 3-8). Instead of speaking of the past historical sufferings of Jesus, the Apostle preferred to emphasize the actuality of Christ's Passion in present Christian life. He insists that, through baptism, the death and resurrection of Jesus have so much become part of each Christian's personal history that, like Jesus, they must ever regard themselves as "dead to sin but alive to God" (cf. Rom. 6, 1-11; Col. 2, 12-13). More than this, Paul makes the Passion of Christ very real for his converts by showing them that, once united to Christ through faith and baptism, they become "another self" for Him. Hence, their trials and difficulties are really "the sufferings of Jesus" if only they share His fidelity to the Father by their own loving obedience to God.

On every page of his Epistles St. Paul manifests a keen sense of the bond that unites all revealed truths and of the eminent importance of each article of faith in practical Christian life. His one concern was to make the saving power of sacred doctrine operative in the lives of his converts. This pastoral orientation and this full confidence in the power of God's word to save and to sanctify are prime requisites for every minister who would lead his flock securely along the ways of God.

LIVING UNITY

It requires only a moment to see how carefully all the articles of faith are to be treasured and how dynamically each of these articles makes its operative contribution to Christian life. It could not be otherwise for all are intimately bound together in the living unity of God's plan for man's salvation. An example will help to emphasize this. The dogma of original sin, with its resultant weakness and tension in every human life (Rom. 7, 14-24), makes one aware of his constant need for the strength and purity of the redeeming blood of Christ if, as a son of Adam, he is to live always as a son of God. What this means becomes clear in the dogma of Mary's Immaculate Conception. Because she was given the grace of Christ in the first moment of her existence and because she was totally faithful to this gift all during her life, her sanctity and loveliness are the perfect model for the spiritual striving of all those who, through baptism, have been re-created in Jesus to the image of God.

Though here we have spoken of only four articles of faith, all the others could be added. God's plan for our salvation is wondrous in its simplicity and unity. Every divine reality in Christian life comes from God's infinite love; and the purpose and power of each reality is to bear man to God. The very person of Jesus, in whom are "all God's treasures of wisdom and knowledge" (Col. 2, 3), makes this clear. Out of His infinite love "God sent His Son . . . to enable us to be adopted as sons" and to utter for all eternity the beautiful word, "Abba," Father (cf. Gal. 4, 4-6).

Therefore, though we recognize a hierarchy in the divine realities which God's word has revealed, a minister of the Gospel must never make light of what some would call a "lesser truth." Every gift of God manifest in the dogmas of sacred doctrine has power to sanctify the Christian; and, in God's providence, some of His "lesser" gifts have had notable impact on the spiritual life of the Church. Thus the glory and prerogatives of Mary, Mother of God, do not rank with the glory of her Son, the Incarnate Word; in the Pauline letters, for instance, Mary is mentioned only once (Gal. 4, 4). However, the fact of history is undeniable that many saints of the Church have found in the Blessed Virgin Mary the most powerful incentive and support for their sanctity. Something similar may be said of another "lesser" dogma, the doctrine of Purgatory. The Church's teaching on the final purification of those who die in Christ touches the heart of the Christian deeply whenever death claims a dear relative or an intimate friend. The dogma of Purgatory, therefore, provides God with one of His most effective means to direct the vision of His children upon earth to their eternal destiny.

Cherishing all the truths of faith, the pastoral minister, like the teacher of the Law in Matthew's Gospel, "is a householder who can produce from his store both the new and the old" (Matt. 13, 52). It is by making use of all the treasures of God's word that a minister will best safeguard and make fruitful the integral word of God in the lives of our Christian people.

4. Sacred Doctrine: the Bond of Unity and Charity

"Fidelity to God's word on the part of minister and people, is the sure guide to that charity and unity which today are shouted from the housetops as the operative themes of true Christianity."

Fidelity to God's word, on the part of minister and people, is the sure guide to that charity and unity which, today, are shouted from the housetops as the operative themes of true Christianity. This contemporary emphasis is so resonant of the teaching of Jesus that striving for

Christian love seems to fulfill all the ideals of authentic Christian life. At times one is tempted to think that charity, no matter how it is understood, and unity, no matter how it is achieved, are the "Open, Sesame" to all that is best in the life of the Church.

All this is true, so long as charity and unity are rightly understood. However, the love of neighbor which the Gospel extols has basic exigencies which some may not see. Even the New Testament, if its separate parts are not read in the context of the whole, could lead one to a myopic understanding of what charity means. The ideals of service, sympathy, concern for the needs of our brother, patience, courtesy and kindliness are so emphasized in the Gospels and Epistles that one may fail to see that all these activities have a distinctive form and finality.

Charity and unity have their only source in the love of God which "is poured forth into our hearts by the Spirit who is given to us" (Rom. 5, 5). But God's love flows from and is identical with the perfect unity of His thought. The Spirit of love proceeds from Father and Son, precisely because the Father begets His Word as the co-equal expression of His divine mind. There could be no Spirit without the Word; there could be no divine love without divine thought. So, too, in all that God has done to save men, His works of love always accord perfectly with the plan and purpose He has revealed in His word and promise. The Prophets of Israel saw this clearly. Each of them follows the lead of the Prophet Hosea in emphasizing that salvation comes not only from God's mercy but also from His total fidelity to His plan and promise. This is the meaning of the phrase which first appears in Hosea and recurs repeatedly in the other Prophets and in the Psalms: *hesed weemeth* (mercy and fidelity). In both Old and New Testaments the living God is not only merciful and compassionate but also rock-like in His unchanging fidelity to the word and promise which manifest His thought and plan: "All the ways of the Lord are mercy and fidelity (*hesed weemeth*) (Ps. 25, 10; cf. *Summa Theol.* Pars. I, Q. 21, art. 4).

This special character of God's love, as something that flows from and is ruled by His thought, provides the form and guideline of Christian charity and unity. To be authentic they must be vital with and characterized by the truth and the plan that are in God. This is what Jesus meant when He prayed, "Father, consecrate them by the *truth;* thy word is *truth* . . . But it is not for these alone (the Apostles) that I pray, but for those also who through their words will believe in me; may they all be one, as thou, Father, art in me and I in thee, so also may they be in us" (Jn. 17, 17-21).

If as Christians, prompted by God's love, we are to minister to the needs of our brothers and to strive for unity with them, our activities must be ruled by the thoughts which God has revealed through His Word. True fellowship (*koinonia*) among men has its source and its rule in true union (*koinonia*) with God, a union with Him which requires perfect fidelity to His word. Repeatedly St. Paul emphasizes that the deeds of Christian service and the striving for Christian unity must all be seen as integral elements of that charity (*agape*) which, like God's love for men, is ruled by the divine thought and word. Thus, in his letter to the Colossians, Paul speaks of this kind of charity as an all-embracing context which alone provides the unifying form for particular deeds of sympathy and service: "You should be clothed in sincere compassion, in kindness and humility, gentleness and patience. Bear with one another; forgive each other . . . And over all these clothes, to keep them together and complete them, put on charity" (Col. 3, 12-14).

For St. Paul the distinctive note in charity is its special finality of helping men to live in accord with God's word. A sentence in his epistle to the Philippians is typical of all his thought. When he appeals to these Christians to be "united in love," he immediately explains that this means they must "be united in their convictions, with a common purpose and a common mind" (Phil. 2, 2). For Paul, this "common mind," as he immediately explains, means total accord with the "mind of Christ." So, too, in his moral recommendations to the Ephesians, he prefaces his directives by affirming that "charity, selflessness, gentleness and patience" must flow from and be based on a total unity of faith (cf. Eph. 4. 1 ff).

Today, when our people have come alive to the pressing need for charity and unity, one may joyfully say that the Church is "ripe for the harvest" of great works for God. But in seeking to strengthen and promote these surges of life the pastoral minister must keep in mind the fundamental truth taught both by Jesus and St. Paul: charity and unity are authentically Christian only when they are ruled by the word of God as delivered to us in the doctrine of the Church. Whereas Marxism is limited to an earth-bound vision of life, the Church cherishes a heavenly vision of man's true destiny to which only the word of God can guide us. For the minister of the Gospel, therefore, the source and rule of his apostolic work must be the firm and abiding conviction that the local church is an authentic Christian community of love only when its people are "of one mind and one heart" in seeking God according to the norms of His word.

In practice, this means that the pastoral ministry of the Church and of every diocese constantly stands under judgment, the judgment of God's word that is "living and active and cuts like any double-edged sword" (Heb. 4, 12). Though the Church and its constituent dioceses should be alive with every kind of pastoral activity, it is even more important that unity of faith and purpose shine radiantly in the rainbow of manifold services and pluriform practices. To safeguard this unity and to strengthen it belong eminently to the charism and responsibility of the Holy Father and the Bishops. Corresponding to this guidance and utilizing their own rich gifts, all other ministers of the Church must strive to build communities of love in which the powerful word of God gives life to true charity and unity.

5. Sacred Doctrine: the Living Word of the Pastoral Ministry

"No price is too great to pay that the Gospel minister may be adept in presenting God's word as the light and life of people's hearts today. This is the very meaning of our ministry in the Church."

Speaking of His own ministry Jesus said, "I have come that men may have life, and may have it in all its fullness" (Jn. 10, 10). These words refer not only to the love with which He gave His life on the cross but also to the solicitude with which He sought to make the word of God a living word in the hearts of men. He who insisted that "God is not the God of the dead but of the living" (Matt. 13, 32) confronted men in the human context of their daily needs, vital concerns, and Palestinian ways of thinking and speaking. In fact, His message was so relevant to His hearers that today careful biblical scholarship is often necessary to determine the precise meaning of His words. As one reads the Gospels one does not know what to admire more—the truth and beauty of Jesus' teaching or His pastoral solicitude to touch the hearts of men with words they could understand and respond to.

The letters of St. Paul reveal the heart of an apostle modelled on the heart of the solicitous Christ. Not only was Paul the faithful spokesman of God's word but, in his ministry, "he became all things to all men that he might gain all for Christ" (cf. 1 Cor. 9, 22). Thus he constantly held up the prism of men's thoughts to the eminent mysteries of God that he might refract into human hearts the rays of light that would warm and transform them. To the Corinthians and Romans, fascinated by the Stoic image of the world as a unified body, Paul explained the mystery of Christian union with Christ and His disciples as the union of the Body and its members. To help men understand what Christ accomplished by His death and resurrection Paul utilized nine different images, all of them familiar to converts who loved to seek out in the Old Testament shadowy anticipations of God's mighty work through His Son. The spectrum of these Pauline images is rich: redemption, expiation, reconciliation, forgiveness, justification, salvation, a new creation, adoption, the Paschal sacrifice. As one marvels at the Apostle's ingenuity he is struck by Paul's solicitude for relevance. In speaking the word of God he kept his eye firmly fixed on the concerns and background of his audience for he knew well that only the word which colors the imagination and warms the heart will bring conviction.

This need for ministry to be relevant is an urgent rule for all apostolate; to be effective the word which ministry speaks must be felt to be a living word. A statement like St. Augustine's, "O Beauty, ever ancient and ever new," may mislead some to a non-Augustinian conclusion. They may think that, so long as an "ancient" truth is expressed, it is bound to have the ring of "newness." The sad result of this conclusion would be dull teaching and boring preaching that would only put people to sleep. Certainly, sacred doctrine, if authentic, is always "ancient"; but the challenge of ministry is to make the age-old truth sound vital and new. If people today say that they believe in God and in Jesus but do not believe in the Church, could it be that some ministers have failed to show them the wonder of Jesus living in the Church to meet their present needs and to illumine their present darkness. This striving for relevance shaped the contents of St. Paul's letters. It is significant that he wrote only twice of man's redemption from original sin (Rom. 5, 12-21; 1 Cor. 15, 21-22); but he wrote numberless times of how Jesus frees men from their personal sins and from the sin-situation in which they live. Could we say that this disproportionate treatment was dictated by Paul's concern to make the redemption meaningful to his readers by showing its effects on the sins of which they were painfully aware?

ENLIGHTENED UNDERSTANDING

An apostle's duty to be relevant demands two things: an enlightened understanding of sacred doctrine, and sensitivity to the preoccupations of men. Often enough sacred doctrine can be expressed in a clear and crisp sentence, as when St. Thomas writes of the Eucharist: "The Eucharist is the sacrament of Christ's Passion according as a man is made perfect in union with Christ who suffered" (S. Theol. III, Q. 73, art. 3, ad 3). But it is the duty of the minister to unfold for his hearers all the heartening truths which St. Thomas has condensed into this brief sentence. With an eye to the needs of people and with the help of the Epistle to the Hebrews, cc. 2 and 5, he has to show that the Jesus who comes to us in the Eucharist is truly our Brother (Heb. 2, 11), who has endured all the testings we must go through here upon earth (Heb. 2, 10; 5, 1-10), and who brings the power of His divinity to strengthen men who are weak, with His own total fidelity to the Father.

Obviously this kind of preaching and teaching requires of the minister both careful study of God's word and careful attention to the language, images and motives which will make God's truth a living power in the hearts of men. Pere de Vaux always taught his students at L'Ecole Biblique in Jerusalem that if someone wanted to have the Bible release its secrets, he had to ponder the text long and prayerfully. In this regard priests could be of great help to one another if they would meet frequently, in small groups, to share their prayerful reflections on a point of sacred doctrine and its relevance to the people among whom they are working. "A brother helped by a brother is like a strong city."

No price is too great to pay that the Gospel minister may be adept in presenting God's word as the light and life of people's hearts today. This is the very meaning of our ministry in the Church; to give Jesus to men in word and sacrament constitutes our priestly identity. Our Holy Father, Pope Paul VI, made this clear in his message of September 27, 1974 to the Synod of Bishops.

"Very often (the sons and daughters of the Church dedicated to apostolic work) are urged to forget the priority that the message of salvation must have, and thus to reduce their own action to mere sociological or political activity, and the message of the Church to a man-centered and temporal message. Hence the need to restate clearly the specifically religious finality of evangelization . . . the kingdom of God, before anything else, in its fully theological meaning, which frees man from sin, and proposes to him love of God as the greatest commandment and as the ultimate destiny of eternal life."

OBJECTIVE MORAL STANDARDS AND PERSONAL RESPONSIBILITY

by Cardinal Hermann Volk
Bishop of Mainz

1. MORAL OBLIGATIONS OF MAN BEFORE GOD

"Man's moral duty arises from the fact that he is bound to God not only in his single acts but also in a deep personal relationship, all the more so since God turned to him unconditionally sending him his Son."

No one can seriously doubt that God makes exacting demands of the Christian. The Old Testament knew the Ten Commandments in the imperative form: "Thou shalt . . .". In the New Testament these commandments have not been abolished, they have rather been reinforced, not through addition to their number, but through the teaching that the commandments are properly observed only when their fulfillment is the expression of love, as is laid down in the chief commandment of love. On these two commandments depend all law and the prophets" (Mt. 22, 40). This does not mean that love has supplanted the other commandments, but that love must inform and characterize their observation. Man's moral duty arises from the fact that he is bound to God not only in his single acts but also in a deep personal relationship, all the more so since God turned to him unconditionally, sending him his Son. *A faith that is fulfilled in love* means unreservedly to answer God's absolute availability. We are all in the position of Peter when the Lord asked him: "Do you love me?" (Jn. 21, 15 ff).

Confronted with this question, we recognize our inadequacy. It is not possible to go to Christ without being saved, without repentance and conversion, as John the Baptist preached. Christ Himself brought to completion his precursor's call to repentance; in his first sermon after the descent of the Holy Ghost, Peter, too, demanded this conversion; "Brethren, what shall we do? And Peter said unto them, Repent, and be baptized every one of you in the name of Jesus Christ for the forgiveness of your sins" (Acts. 2, 37 ff).

In his letter to the Galatians, Paul warns: "For you were called to freedom, brethren; only do not use your freedom as an opportunity for the flesh, but through love be servants of one another" (Gal. 5, 13). Here, in fact, is described the irreconcilable opposition between the flesh and the spirit, the spirit representing the disposition towards God in active faith, the flesh the withdrawal within himself of the man estranged from God. To the New Testament catalogue of vices, Paul adds: "I warn you, as I warned you before, that those who do such things shall not inherit the kingdom of God" (Gal. 5, 21).

TOTAL DISREGARD

But repentance is necessary not only for conversion to the faith, but also for the deepening of faith and love. For resolute turning to God entails resolute renunciation of self, as Christ unsurpassingly accomplished it in renunciation of self-exaltation and of any manifestation of power in his favor. But it was in this total disregard of himself and in full adherence to the Father's will that Christ fully accomplished his mission. "Therefore God has highly exalted him, and bestowed on him the name which is above every name" (Phil 2, 9). And this is the inalienable structure of Christian life: to disregard oneself more and more and to aim more and more at conformity with Christ, which is man's consummation.

We are, therefore, obliged to seek Christ unreservedly, out of love, and the Father in Christ. Yet we know that man can sin, and in varying degrees of culpability up to mortal sin, which prevents him from taking part in the kingdom of God. The penitential practice of the Church, that is the condition for the remission of the sins of the baptized, was very severe in the first centuries. The problem raised was not specifically whether even the sins of the baptized could be forgiven but whether the baptized who had sinned grievously, were capable once more of repentance and conversion. Only when it had been established that even the believer who had become a sinner was capable of real repentance, did the practice of penance become firmly established.

2. Church's Teaching on Moral Duty

"The Church is concerned not only with doctrine, but also the acceptance of the doctrine as an obligation which the individual really feels."

An important and inalienable task of the Church is to substantiate and justify the moral obligations incumbent on the faithful. Conversion to Christ in repentance and faith must be concretely expressed. "Let us not love in word or speech but in deed and in truth" (1 Jn. 3, 18). If faith is not expressed in action and in life, salvation might be lost. The Church, therefore, must describe and substantiate life in faith and through faith.

The nature of the Christian's moral obligation cannot, however, be entirely deduced from Holy Scripture; the Scripture does not speak of everything, or it does so in so general a fashion that it needs to be concretized. And for this purpose theological science and, in particular, moral theology are necessary, in order to be able to deduce or interpret concrete cases from general assumptions, always in conformity with the teachings of the ecclesiastical Magisterium. The letter to the Romans says in this connection that the Gentiles, who do not possess the Mosaic Law "are a law unto themselves; in that they show the work of the law written in their hearts, their conscience bearing witness therewith" (Rom. 2, 15). Actually, men, in their inclination to sin, have overturned the demands of the law and its contents; they are almost slaves of this inclination to sinfulness. However, even if the perfect knowledge of our moral duty comes to us from Holy Scripture, we must recognize that the first knowledge emerges from man's being. From the beginning of Christianity a great deal, both in theory and practice, has been accomplished in this respect; the lesson of the Saints cannot be overlooked. On the other hand renewed effort is more and more necessary in the field of theology, also because there are new problems. As an example, we can mention the question of usury and its various solutions; the issue of the justification of war has been brought up again more urgently, particularly atomic war or war carried out with other modern means of destruction. We are confronted with the problems involved in the development of peoples, with the question whether the economic and social structures are the right ones, and the responsibility of rich men and peoples for the greater part of mankind, who are in want.

Further theological study may also be necessary to reinforce and deepen the basis of the early Church's moral teaching. The Church is concerned not only with the doctrine, but also with the acceptance of the doctrine as an obligation which the individual really feels. In this connection a new concern may become necessary. Since we all live not only in the Church but also in the world, we are, to a certain extent, influenced by the thinking and way of life of the world, of man in the world. Today, the world is abandoning moral standards very hastily in some sectors. The Christian experiences this process. Therefore he is inevitably confronted with the question of whether, and how far, he can identify himself with it. The Christian must win growing independence from the world. "Do not be conformed to this world but be transformed by the renewal of your mind, that you may prove what is the will of God, what is good and acceptable and perfect" (Rom. 12, 2). While necessarily distancing himself from the world, the Christian, however, must not become increasingly isolated; he must rather find support for his Christian way of life in the community of the faithful by means of the doctrine of the Church and finally by means of the Church herself. The need to achieve distance and win independence from the world must not, therefore, lead to a corresponding independence and distance with regard to the Church. The Christian makes himself more independent of the world the more resolutely he takes up position within the Church, attaching himself to her and through her to Christ.

3. Uncertainties over moral evaluation of action

It cannot be ignored that there is noticeable uncertainty today over the binding force of the Church's moral teaching. Science poses new and specific questions and at the same time the reception and acceptance of the Church's teaching among the faithful has fallen into uncertainty through a consciousness of the difference between defined and undefined dogma.

Psychology, among the sciences, has questioned whether the premises and subjective conditions for grievous sin are, in fact, present as often as has been, and is, commonly stated. On the basis of the Bible, the question is raised whether the right stresses have been laid in the conception of the duties of Christian life worked out and preserved by the teaching of the Church, and precisely whether injustice, violation of human rights, violence, absence of love and similar conduct have been and are sufficiently clearly branded as un-Christian. Today the question is also posed whether commandments and laws are universally valid, so that they are invariably binding on each believer, everywhere.

It is recognized that there exist commandments that are ordinarily binding. It is also recognized that the Church has the task of validating emphatically her own moral doctrine. Difficulties, however, are encountered in putting the commandment and the common law into practice. It is a question, substantially, of the general commandment as an objective standard and of the subjective conscience of the individual.

It cannot be considered a priori that under these questions there is a tendency to weaken the general validity or binding force of God's commandments. And yet this tendency exists. The fear of God which, according to Scripture is "the beginning of wisdom" (Prov. 1, 7: Acts 9, 31; 2 Cor. 7, 1) is rarely invoked nowadays. In fact, there is a whole range of problems in this field with which moral theology is concerned. We must first of all indicate the assumptions on which the question as to whether the general commandment is absolutely binding on the individual in every case, can legitimately be posed. The assumptions underlying the obligatory character of the moral law must therefore be indicated.

4. General principles and the individual case

The moral character of a human act depends on the content of the act itself, the intention of the author, and the circumstances which contribute to its moral qualification. A great many important things have been said about these three necessary aspects of human action—above all, the fact that the content of the act is determining for its moral qualification. But the act is not independent of the subject; in his freedom to act, man is the responsible agent, the subject of his conduct. Purpose, therefore, comes to have moral validity, without however making it possible for evil conduct to be legitimized by good purpose. Good intentions do not justify evil means, and vice versa. Even the most diverse immediate circumstances of an act contribute to its ethical character. This is not surprising. Man is always more than his being; human conduct is always more than its substance. In man there are always elements which are not intrinsic to his essential being. For since man exists and acts in history, and therefore in ever-changing situations, human conduct must inevitably take place under ever different circumstances. Man can have a variety of relationships with his environment and with other men, he can and must act under very different circumstances and inner conditions.

Uncertainty over the conception of the human being or his nature and growing awareness of deep change, both in the course of history and in the present, in the circumstances under which man must act responsibly and morally, have also led to the doubt that the moral law may be subject to change.

It is necessary to speak about this in order to clarify the problem of the relationship between objective moral standards and the subjective conscience, without prejudicing in any way the value of moral standards on the one hand and that of individual conscience on the other hand.

5. Nature or person as standard: a false alternative

Today the explanation of man drawn from his being, his nature, from which general obligatory moral laws are allegedly deducible, does not enjoy much credit. Nature is now chiefly understood in the sense of the natural sciences; but it is not this concept of nature that can be understood as the standard of moral conduct. But the term *"man's nature"* is not clear either. According to some people, it would be more apposite to speak here of *man's being*, though its identification with substance again poses problems in contemporary thought.

But also the interpretation of the idea of *nature* or *being* as the foundation of ethics and the natural law has been made more difficult by the ruling personalism of our time. Actually, one cannot but wonder if it is not better to use the concept of *person* rather than *nature* or *being*, in theological language. It may not be easy, in fact, to consider man's being or nature as the moral subject and the responsible agent of moral decision. The moral subject is the person, and precisely the human person, man as person. For it is the *person* that is addressed in God's revelation and in the proclamation of the faith; it is the *person* that is loved, and it is the person that must answer, responsibly, in love. But the person is unique, unexchangeable, unrepeatable. No two persons are the same. The specific nature, on the other hand, the essence, what makes man a man, is repeatable; it is the same in all men, and serves as the basis for the same general obligation. The person, on the contrary, varies from man to man. If the objective standard of morality is deduced only from the essence, which is one and the same, and therefore the moral standard indicates how man must behave solely on the basis of his nature, then the objective norm has an absolute validity, without admitting exceptions; if, on the contrary, morality is referred also to the individual person in his uniqueness, then generalizations are not such as not to admit of exceptions.

At this point three questions arise. Firstly, whether nature is so uniform and constant that it holds validity for everyone in the same way. In the Middle Ages this question was clearly posed and hotly debated in terms of the doctrine of universals. It was recognized that there must be something in common, *man's being,* otherwise the absurd conclusion would be reached that not all men are men.

The second question is whether Christian duty can also find its foundation, for the most part, in man's nature. It should be noted, in connection with this problem, that the order of salvation is contingent on the order of creation and that which comes from Christ transforms but does not suppress what arises from man's nature as a creature. Furthermore, one must be certain that in the direction *from* and *towards* Christ no harm is ever done to man's nature or being, even when, for example, the evanglical precepts of poverty, obedience and celibacy are accepted "for love of the kingdom of heaven." In Christ, the evangelical precepts are a legitimate mode of Christian life, and they do not diminish man's nature.

The third question is if the alternative—whether it is common nature or the unique and unrepeatable person that should provide the standard of moral law and conduct—is justified. No, this alternative is not justified. Because man's reality does not exist as a *something,* man is always personal, so that in him matter stops being *"something"*; in man matter is personified. On the other hand, there is no such thing as a person without a substance suitable for being a person. Frequently, when we say *person*, we also mean *nature*, and vice versa, because the one cannot materially exist without the other. Thus the alternative *nature* or *person* is false; it does not exist.

6. The personal being of man as the foundation of moral standards

"Today man's awareness of himself emphasizes the differences between men at the expense of what they have in common."

The indissoluble connection between person and nature makes objective and general standards possible and convincing. The person can reach completion, that is, be that which he must be, only through relationship with other persons and finally with God. One step forward is that man is now considered in theological terms as a person and not as an individual. *Relationships* form an essential part of our present understanding of personality. This conforms to the theological interpretation of man, whose likeness to God does not mean in itself independence, but a personal, binding and hence normative relationship of obedience to God.

With this there coincides the fact that the person is not conceived as being so unique that general obligatory standards of morality of general validity would, on the grounds of nature or substance, be impossible. Certainly, however, the general validity of objective standards is sometimes questioned not only on grounds of the uniqueness of the person, but also on grounds of difference in substance. Men are differentiated, in fact, not only by the uniqueness of the person but also by differences in temperament, heredity, capacity, and the situations in which men must act. Today our awareness of this emphasizes the differences between men at the expense of what they have in common; our consciousness of history makes us perceive almost only change, and not continuity in the sense of authentic tradition; we see only what is different in humanity and not what there is in common or the same. Today mankind recognizes itself as a whole, but, it is more disposed to note differences on the grounds of race, culture and tradition than what is held in common. Psychology, too, puts the emphasis rather on the diversity of men. All this makes it more difficult to present and recognize general and objective standards of morality.

In spite of all this, objective moral standards binding on all do exist. This cannot be demonstrated by denying the deep-seated differences between men. It can only be demonstrated by stressing the common element there is in the person. It is an unquestionable fact that all men must have something in common. This essential truth needs to be studied more deeply on the philosophical plane from a great many points of view but it cannot be ignored.

Theology, too, offers arguments to demonstrate the *unity of man*. The decisive theological argument is the following: the one and same Jesus of Nazareth is, for all men, Christ, the Savior, with all the essential prerogatives of human nature itself since he is the Son of God *made man*. Christ is the Head of all men, the second and more authentic Adam. This includes and presumes human creation, the solidarity of men in the need for salvation, God's call in revelation and salvation for all. Through Christ there arise relationships which cannot be founded only in the uniformity of being; they have the character of mysteries, and are founded exclusively in Christ's unifying power; but they presume the unity or uniformity of the human being. In Holy Scripture we have, in fact, a plurality of authors and recipients; nevertheless it has unity because Christ's message is one and applies to all men of all times. Therefore, to make the assumptions clear means also to make clear the grounds for objective, universally binding moral standards. This is important in our times because not infrequently there seems to be a tendency to take decisions in the opposite direction.

7. Subjective decision contrary to general standard

It must be admitted that cases of this kind may occur. This does not justify us, however, in thinking that the objecive norm is not, in itself and generally, valid and binding, but rather that the conditions in the subject are so changed or so particular as to prevent him from recognizing the general law or make him think that the general law does not apply in that particular case. Every subject has, furthermore, the duty of doing his utmost to know the objective standard and act in accordance with it. The teachings of the ecclesiastical Magisterium are a light and guidance for this purpose, and must be given religious assent.

While it must be recognized that, in some cases, it is possible to be subjectively right in acting against the general law, it is undeniable that real "good" can be reached, even from the personal and subjective standpoint, only by faithful observance of this objective law.

8. Beyond the general law

It should be recalled, too, that the individual can be morally bound *beyond* the requirement of the general standard.

The incentive to go beyond general morality springs in essence from the chief commandment, love as the answer to God's unconditional love for us. For God not only loves, He is love, not in words, but in deed and in truth, as was revealed in Jesus Christ. And since faith is completed only in love, thus bearing fruits of good works, it is "the obedience of faith" (Rom. 1, 5-16, 26) that the person should put himself completely at the disposal of Christ and in Christ of the Father. Now the possibilities of expressing all this concretely are not limited to the general law.

It is therefore a necessary and indispensable task of the Church to describe and substantiate not only moral obligations, but also the believer's moral possibilities of going beyond what is strictly his duty. The Church, therefore, must not only indicate what is in conflict with the Kingdom of God and the salvation of man; it is also her task to describe what possibilities are offered to the Christian to realize fully the Kingdom of God on earth, to carry out his mission in the world. Many Christians are called upon to do more than that which is strictly obligatory, according to general moral laws. This necessity—of *doing more, of not limiting ourselves to a minimum requirement*—is of crucial importance, since we ought in our conduct to reciprocate God's conduct in Christ towards us and in imitation of Christ himself. Christ did not ask what was required of him, but what He could do for us. And so we too ought to do not only what is absolutely necessary, but what we are able to do, in imitation of Christ. For love does not ask what must be done; it asks what can be done. We find this not only in Christ's example but also in the teachings of Holy Scripture. The Sermon on the Mount could hardly be interpreted as a general obligatory law, but rather as a pressing opportunity and also as a task of the Christian, the implementation of which is entrusted to him with the aid of divine grace. This is made quite clear in the story of the rich young man: "If you would be perfect, go, sell what you possess and give it to the poor and you will have treasure in heaven; then come, follow me" (Mt. 19, 21). The same thing is said of celibacy for the sake of the Kingdom of Heaven (Mt. 19, 12).

The Christian is called upon to do more than what is obligatory for everyone. The Christian can do more because the chief commandment is love. But all that love can do (cf. 1 Cor. 13) cannot be encompassed in general laws and standards. Therefore each individual must ask himself what is expected of him, now, in the imitation of Christ, as witness of Christ and in building the Kingdom of God.

The Christian, therefore, can be called to do *more* than what is enjoined on him by the general moral law. In this connection, our age is in the process of de-christianization, departing more and more from Christian moral standards and principles. Consequently, humanity is being secularized not only in the legitimate sense of the recognition of the specific value that *things* have, but also in a quite illegitimate sense. For in breaking away from Christ, mankind is not returning to a spirit of expectation and simple faith in God; it very soon withdraws within itself, and certainly not only in its successes, but also in its lack of hope and despair. The world is becoming a secular world: creation denying the Creator. And the growth of this perverted, extreme secularization must be opposed not with adaptation to the world but with increased conformity to Christ as witness of what ought to be. This, too, admits of no minimalism; the question we must ask, first of all, is not *what must I not do,* but *what can I do* in imitation of Christ, in accordance with the change of heart in the Holy Spirit.

Finally, the individual, when acting, must ask himself if his behavior will be held up as an example, will win support or give offence. These circumstances must be recognized as a challenge to intensifying the obligation. The world is becoming increasingly secularized, it recognizes Christian standards less and less. So the responsibility of respecting the standards and also of opening one's heart *beyond* the standards, also increases. Circumstances thus demand the intensification of specifically Christian responses. We must be ready to give them without fear of being more tied down as a result. For we do not understand concrete and uncompromising attachment to God in the imitation of Christ as a limitation of the person. Christ came directly to fullness in his absolute obedience to the heavenly Father's will. Abraham, too, preferred the obedience of faith, against all appearances, to his own calculations. Freedom culminates not in the absence of restraints, not in being ready to fall back even before God, but rather in the decision to bind oneself to God. At a time when the task of the Christian towards his brothers, in the faith and in the world, is emphasized particularly, the responsibility of violating the general standard from personal motivation is particularly great. For what has to be done in the present situation is to strengthen brothers in the faith and in the obedience of faith, and to indicate to the world liberation and freedom with their rightful and indispensable obligations.

THE CHURCH AT THE SERVICE OF MANKIND

by Fr. Umberto Betti, O.F.M.

PROFESSOR AT THE PONTIFICAL UNIVERSITY "ANTONIANUM"

Today the world is in the throes of a crisis of growth and a growth of anxieties.

Man has embarked on a movement of complete liberation. To wider understanding of the mysteries of the universe and his own mystery there corresponds a more marked self-sufficiency of thought and a more complacent narcissism of self-determination. The satisfaction of his aspirations, which still torment him, in spite of everything, is not postponed to a hypothetical day of God that is to come; he expects it from man's day that has already arrived. To an equally hypothetical redemption coming from outside, he prefers a "lay" redemption, which he can carry out by himself, by activating and harnessing the energies immanent in nature.

It seems, therefore, that the modern world shuns all contact of necessity with the Church. It refuses her saving influence, and even contests her presence; and with all the impetus of hopes considered to have been deceived hitherto.

Yet the Church has always manifested what her intentions are, nor could she do otherwise. She claims not so much the right as the duty to exist as the witness of God who saves, considering that the absence of this witness would be the most serious mutilation of man. More than an existence, or even a coexistence, hers is a pro-existence in the world: a being, that is, in the service of men; an offer of friendship to one and all.

In all its documents, the Second Vatican Council, more or less deliberately, and more clearly than in the past, repeated those intentions obliging the Church to new and also unprecedented attitudes towards the world of today in its cultural, social and historical reality. The Church summarizes these attitudes in the declaration that she wishes to be "in favor and in the service of men," giving the exact and sublime interpretation of man "by virtue of her knowledge of God" (Paul VI, Conciliar address, December 7, 1965: *Insegnamenti di Paolo VI,* III, p. 731).

This renewed declaration of the Church, that she is in the service of mankind, calls for some reflection on the theological foundations which contribute to guiding its orderly implementation. Though with a certain conventionality, they can be indicated in the threefold relationship of the Church with the world, sustained by corresponding principles with the same denomination: relationship of communion; relationship of autonomy; relationship of transcendency.

The meaning and the limits of each are rooted in a consideration that embraces them all. It is the following: the Church has a purpose of salvation that can be fully attained only beyond her earthly phase; her mission on earth is "supremely human" since it is essentially religious (cf. Vat. Council II, Past. Constit. *Gaudium et Spes*, n. 11); consequently, the interpenetration of the Church and the world can be perceived only with faith (cf. *l.c.*, n. 40).

1. Relationship of Communion

The Church unites her voice with the voice of the world to recognize together those of its elements that are valid on the human plane, and offers her own contribution to complete them.

Since the Church has her historical origin in Christ, the incarnation of God is the type and the cause of her peculiar relationship with the world.

God, becoming man, entered visibly and irreversibly into the order of his creation, to "re-establish all things in Christ" (Eph. 1, 10). In Christ, therefore, presence and action of the one definitive salvation, men reacquire the capacity of being saved, which had been lost by the first sin. And the whole of creation, in him creator and creature, participates in its own way in the capacity of cooperating with God in man's salvation.

The Church is the attestation and proclamation of God's presence among men in order to save them where and as they are.

As in Christ God is in mankind and mankind is assumed in God, so the Church is in the world and the world is in the Church, made up of men who remain in the worldly condition in which they were when they were called (cf. 1 Cor. 7, 24). She finds herself, therefore, in a relationship of communion with the world, communion based on reciprocity of interests and experiences.

Her title as People of God does not make her a sect of segregated beings. The segregation inherent in every divine choice is expressed for the Church in the mission "of announcing the Gospel of God" (Rom. 1, 1). Since she was assumed by Christ to be the instrument of the redemption of all, she is sent by him to the world (cf. Second Vat. Council, Dogmatic Constit. *Lumen Gentium*, n. 9) as a community of men among men, a living organ of his presence in their midst (cf. Jn. 17, 18).

The title, furthermore, of sacrament of union with God and of the unity of all mankind (cf. Second Vat. Council, Dogmatic Constit. *Lumen Gentium*, n. 1) constitutes for the Church the constitutional necessity of taking her place fully in all the structures of society, though with her own specific message which enables her to manifest the unifying force of which she is the bearer and the sign.

The Church carries out her mission of presence in a more immediate way, in the form of anamnesis: that is, by reviving the memory of what the world has been hitherto.

In the first place the memory of the divine origin of all things. This is inscribed in the initial creative act, which is prolonged in the new aspects imprinted upon them by the events of history and man's genius. For the very reason that they were created and preserved by God by means of the Word, a perennial divine testimony is offered to men in them all (of Second Vat. Council, Dogmatic Constit. *Dei Verbum*, n. 3). This testimony became transparent in Christ, so much so that anyone who sees him sees the Father (cf. Jn. 14, 9); and is communicated by Christ to all men, to the extent that He considers as done for himself what is done for the least of his brethren (cf. Mt. 25, 40).

Then the memory of the past. Not as an "alibi" to shun commitment in the present, but to remind mankind as it is today what it owes, not only to God, but to the men of the past.

To the revived memory of the origins and of the past, the Church also gives an expression of worship as the affirmation of humanity. It is part of the completeness of human nature, in fact, to show gratitude for what it has received from God and from men. The Eucharist it celebrates signifies and effects the unity of the People of God (cf. Vat. Council II, Dogmatic Constit. *Lumen Gentium*, n. 11): and this unity, in its turn, is a "leaven of brotherly cohesion in the community of peoples" (Paul VI, Apost. Exhortation *Paterna cum benevolentia*, December 8, 1974, n. 2). That celebration of the Church, therefore, is a permanent stimulus to men to put themselves, too, in the "eucharistic" dimension of thanksgiving, which will free them from short-lived self-complacency and open up to them wider frontiers of space and time.

In this perspective the Church unites her voice with the voice of the world, to recognize together those of its elements that are valid on the human plane, and offers her own contribution to complete them, since they are human. She does not claim to be the exclusive holder of patents of goodness, as if she considered true goods those belonging to her specifically, and false goods those extraneous to her specific sphere. She recognizes, on the contrary, that there exist goods without further qualification, bestowed upon herself and upon the world by the same munificence of God.

The Church, therefore, promotes and protects all improvement of man and of the world, seeing in every value of creation also an evangelical value. For this purpose, she respects the diversities peculiar to each one, taken individually or considered in the plurality of forms of associated life, because she considers them the most suitable means to favor all human maturation. For the same reason, she does not bind herself to any particular culture, because she considers them all perfectible and at the same time perfecting, and for this reason converging in one authentically human civilization; which, in order to be such, must be accessible and communicable to all. Participating, furthermore, in joint initiatives in all sectors and at all levels, of a cultural and religious nature, as well as of social and diplomatic significance, she is convinced that she is carrying out a real ecclesial service, ordained as it is to the full promotion of every man and the whole man. This participation can also include positions of open dissent, when the Church remains practically alone in defending values which she judges to be intrinsically human, such, for example, as those connected with the transmission and protection of life.

In a word, the Church maintains a relationship of communion with the world in that she is an "expert in humanity" (cf. Paul VI, Message to U.N., October 4, 1965: *Insegnamenti,* III, p. 517), in order to contribute to keeping it human, and to preserve it from factors that insulate or injure its original dignity. This is a requirement of faithfulness to her mission and her doctrine, even if her mission of salvation cannot stop here.

2. Relationship of Autonomy

The Church must remain spiritually independent of the systems and methods of purely human structures which, however valid and proportionate to their immediate purpose are only partly effective for the purposes of her mission of salvation.

Although the Church is on a plane of existential parity among worldly realities, yet she has her own ontological constitution and mission of salvation which distinguish her from any other.

God created the world out of love, humbling himself, in a certain sense, by the mere fact of giving, He the infinite, existence to the finite. At the origin of the Church in Christ there is a new creative act; and that first divine humiliation is brought to the limit of renunciation, to the extent of becoming "kenosis": God so loved the world that He gave his only begotten Son to save it (cf. Jn. 3, 16); He emptied himself, taking the form of a servant, being born in the likeness of men (cf. Phil. 2, 7), except for sin (cf. Heb. 4, 15). Since, therefore, the Church is derived from an extraordinary constitutive initiative of God, her existence is not a postulate of the creature essence of the world. It is an autonomous existence.

To autonomy of origin is added autonomy of mission. The latter is carried out in the world beset by the alienating forces of sin which put it "in the power of evil" (1 Jn. 5, 19), and cancel all interior distinction between men, "since all have sinned and fall short of the glory of God" (Rom. 3, 23). Although the Church, unlike Christ who did not know sin, is at the same time holy and always in need of purification (cf. II Vat.

Council, Dogmatic Constit. *Lumen Gentium,* n. 8), she is, however, assumed by Him as the instrument of the redemptoin of all and, as such, to operate so that they may become God's slaves again (cf. Rom. 6, 22). The service that she is called to carry out, therefore, is a service of liberation; and, in the first place, on the religious plane.

It is a liberating service, which aims at bringing men back from the unnatural condition in which they find themselves because of sin, to the condition for which God created them, which is the state of friendship with him. It follows that the Church must remain spiritually independent of the systems and methods of purely human structures which, however valid and proportionate to their immediate purpose, are only partly effective for the purposes of her mission of salvation. It is part, therefore, of the purpose of her mission to exercise a critical function with regard to the temporal order, with the aim not of absorbing but of correcting the latter, without, however, altering its specific nature.

It is, furthermore, a service of a specifically religious nature. Sin, after all, is also a religious reality. Not only because it overthrew God's plan; but also because God, in order to put right the disorder derived from it, established a personal contact with sin itself, "for our sake making Christ to be sin" (2 Cor. 5, 21). It is, therefore, the primary task of the Church to communicate Christ and his Gospel to the world as a measure and comparison of human behavior with God's judgment.

A critical function, therefore, it requires the Church to be a witness of the discrimination between good and evil, judging them both by their impact on man's salvation. This is the idea on which the whole Gospel is based. The division indicated by Christ as the *raison d'etre* of his presence in the world (cf. Mt. 10, 34s: Lk. 12, 51), runs through the whole of history; and it will be concluded with the definitive separation when all nations are gathered before the Son of man, and He "will separate them one from another as a shepherd separates the sheep from the goats" (Mt. 25, 32).

CRITICAL FUNCTION

This critical function has a twofold point of reference. On the one hand there is divine Revelation, which must be maintained in its specificity and normatve sovereignty. On the other hand there is the contemporary presence of the Church at every moment and expression of human existence, which enables her to examine the signs of the times and interpret them in the light of the Gospel, thus replying to men's questions in a way adapted to every generation (cf. II Vat. Council, *Gaudium et Spes,* n. 4; cf. also n. 11). By means of this evangelical penetration from within, she is able to pick up the divine waves present in the phenomena characteristic of every age. They reveal the dangers concealed in those phenomena and encourage the opportunities they have to offer.

By so doing the Church does not engage in a work of obscurantism, as if spreading a pall of opaqueness over the world, as one might think who renounces a sincere effort of thought at the outset. On the contrary: she assiduously explores the light which, radiating from the Gospel into the world, also shines in the darkness, a darkness that is not able to overcome it (cf. Jn. 1, 5).

It has furthermore a more directly religious function. This consists in ensuring that the presence of God, which can be felt more or less at all levels of experience will reach man's inner life and restore him to his complete authenticity as a creature of God redeemed by Christ.

For this purpose the Church proposes to men a type of fully rehabilitated humanity; and points to Christ as the principle and model which guarantees that this rehabilitation will take place. When Christ proposes the cross as the condition of discipleship (cf. Mt. 16, 24; Mk. 8, 34; Lk. 14, 27), he is not alluding to mere resignation before superficial difficulties. He demands a free choice which involves also secret intentions: the choice of belonging to him by means of the crucifixion of one's passions and desires (cf. Gal. 5, 24), which can "transform into an instrument of sin those human energies intended for the service of God and man" (*Gaudium et Spes,* n. 37). Just as it was necessary for Christ to suffer to enter into his glory (cf. Lk. 24, 26), so men must take a penitential path which, separating them from the mentality of this world, will transform them inwardly, and in this way they will be able to discern God's will (cf. Rom. 12, 2).

This proclamation of Christ, and Christ crucified, does not put the Church in a situation of conflict with mankind; because the event of God who became man and died for man's salvation is part of humanity itself, and is the permanent attestation of the love with which He loved the world. It puts mankind, however, in a state of dynamic tension, intended to ensure that that love will be requited, giving men the awareness that their activities, daily endangered by sin, must be purified and made perfect by means of the cross and the resurrection of Christ (cf. *Gaudium et Spes, ibid.*) and so that all humanity will be drawn to him in this way (cf. Jn. 12, 32).

That dynamic tension, moreover, is reflected on the Church herself, obliging her to that congenital anticonformism which constitutes the status of full freedom given her by Christ, who "for freedom has set us free" (Gal. 5, 1).

Consequently, the validity of her presence and action in the world is bound up exclusively with the complete application of the revealed message of which she is the depositary and the interpreter. Any compromise reducing the Gospel to please men would be a renunciation of their real service, because it would be an abdication from Christ's service (cf. Gal. 1, 10). If the Gospel were dissolved into a cultural or social or political ideology, with the consequent reduction of faith to a mere religious ethics or pragmatic cooperation, the contribution of the Church to the progress of mankind, if not completely superfluous, would certainly not be original or creative. In fact, after an ambiguous welcome, which is usually granted more to weight of numbers than to the force of truth, it would be judged as an attack, though an unsuccessful one, upon the inalienable autonomy of the temporal order.

To remain herself, the Church, though operating in the horizontal dimension, cannot break away from the verticality of her matrix and purpose. She cannot, therefore, seek self-realization in the immediate results of her action nor identify herself with the latter. Hers is, necessarily, a history also of failures, in the face of which she has no other recourse than to the pride that Christ commanded her to have: "And if any place will not receive you and they refuse to hear you, when you leave, shake off the dust that is on your feet for a testimony against them" (Mk. 6, 11). This is not a gesture of contempt for mankind. It is the profession of the desire to serve men with the humility of leaven (cf. Mt. 13, 33; Lk. 13, 21), which takes a long time to transform flour into bread.

3. Relationship of Transcendency

This proclamation of the primacy of what is beyond time is not a reason for anyone to flee from, or take no interest in, human problems that call for immediate solutions. It rather bids us to give them the best solution, which will prepare the definitive solution, almost anticipating it.

The Church's service for humanity always remains incomplete, because humanity itself is incomplete and the Church is also incomplete.

No created reality acquires fixed stability. They are all driven to peer beyond the limits of time by the very force of their temporal nature, deriving from the creative act that made them such. Even death is only apparently the annihilation of man; in fact it is an ontological component, and therefore a moment of life. The Church herself, here on earth, is only the germ and the beginning of the Kingdom of God, which is slowly growing towards its fullness. Even in her sacraments and her institutions, which belong to the present age, she is endued with the fleeting figure of this world (cf. *Lumen Gentium,* nn. 5 and 48).

The whole of creation, in a word, is involved in a process of purification and transfiguration "until the time of the restoration of all things, when all creatures will meet again with Christ, the first born of the risen dead" (Paul VI, *Paterna cum benevolentia,* n. 2).

The Church, according to the logic of the scale of values and in faithfulness to her transcendency of origin, and mission, has the task of affirming the primacy of the future, which will be the fulfillment, for creation, of the hope of being freed from futility to which it has been subjected by God (cf. Rom. 8, 19-21).

This proclamation of the primacy of what is beyond time is not a reason for anyone to flee from, or take no interest in, human problems that call for immediate solutions. It rather bids us give them the best solution, which will prepare the definitive solution, almost anticipating it. Holiness, too, to be fully Christian, must be fully human; it must derive from a "manner of life worthy of the gospel of Christ" (Phil. 1, 27) during this present life. In this connection an eloquent reminder comes from the liturgy of this Lenten period, which is intended as an initiation to the resurrection of Easter: let the faithful "live in this earthly life, with their gaze ever directed towards the eternal life" (Preface II).

So the expectation of the future, which the Church announces as a guideline of the present, is, as it were, an epiclesis fecundating all the seeds of eternity enclosed in time. And this is a stimulus and support for that great and energetic hope that pervades the world, in spite of everything, and which—as the Pope said recently—"seems to interpret the prophecy of history: the world can renew itself, again and always" (*L'Osservatore Romano*, English edition, January 30, 1975; p. 1, col. 1).

REFLECTION ON THE PROBLEM OF PLURALISM IN THE CHURCH

by Mons. Philippe Delhaye

SECRETARY OF THE INTERNATIONAL COMMISSION
PROFESSOR AT THE UNIVERSITY OF LOUVAIN

1. The purpose of this article

Our intention is to present here some information and some reflections on pluralism in the Church such as the problem is raised today. The word pluralism nearly always causes a shock; when you give lectures on this subject, you are almost certain that it will arouse enthusiasm in some, hostility in others.

Twenty years ago, perhaps, the term "pluralism" had a very precise meaning in philosophy: it denoted the systems of thought that recognized a plurality of being in opposition to monism which saw in things and men mere exterior and deceptive manifestations of one reality[1]. In that case, practically everyone was a pluralist! But in the last few years there has been a clear semantic evolution and pluralism now presents itself as a claim for diversity, reaching the point of heterogeneity, if necessary, both on the geographical plane and on the historical plane. From a pluralist civil society in which various religions coexist peacefully[2], we arrive more or less at the point of speaking of pluralism in the Church to try to justify serious divergences in the field of faith and morality[3].

RAPID CHANGE

That language should evolve, is a natural fact, especially at a time of rapid change such as is the case today. But it must be clearly seen also that this evolution may be a trap: let us recognize this without gloominess or pessimism but with lucidity. Apparently, it is harmless to replace the word "abortion" with "interruption of pregnancy." But from the evoluton of polemics on this painful subject, it can be seen that this is prompted by the desire to set aside a word that traditionally connotes reprobation in favor of another which opens the door to attempts at legitimization. The same holds good with regard to the word "morality." To begin with, people dared not attack it directly, in spite of the difficulties that morality always brings with it as a result of the effort and asceticism, even the renunciations, that it involves. "Moralism," which condemned certain excesses, was called into question, just as it was attempted in the past to combat "Augustinianism" by pretending to confuse it with Jansenism, the errors of which were recognized. Once "morality" was discredited by its closeness to "moralism," other formulas were brought forward to replace it: "ethics," "ethos," "praxis," etc. They may be harmless and perfectly acceptable in the sense that some people give them but in most cases they imply an evolution from "right" (what must be done) to "fact" (how people live in practice) or else the passing from a normative science implying an obligation to a purely descriptive sociology.

PRESENT CRISIS

This means that we will have to distinguish very carefully the different meanings of the term "pluralism" and even more the different fields to which it is desired to apply it. But for this same purpose it is important to look for the reasons why man now towards the end of the 20th century is so fascinated by pluralism in any area whatsoever. We would be wrong to envisage the present religious crisis as a "hortus conclusus"; it is actually bound up with a whole crisis of civilization[4]. The students who enter a theology faculty have studied Hegel, Husserl, Heidegger, and they apply their cast of mind to the religious sciences. The faithful who listen to the homilies of their parish priests and who study the teaching of the Magisterium, are also men whose way of thinking and feeling has been remodelled by the mass media. TV and radio in the different countries of the world create an outlook and an opinion that compel recognition all the more so in that most listeners are unaccustomed to think for themselves or, at the end of a day's work, too tired to do so.

Many readers are probably aware that the international theological Commission studied the problems of pluralism for several years. They are perhaps acquainted with the volume on its work which was published in 1973[5]. They might be afraid that I am merely summarizing this volume here. I wish to reassure them. For, from the work carried out until 1973, I would like, on the contrary, to take into account the evolution of the problem. This evolution is particularly clear in the first place on the plane of psycho-sociology and philosophy, revealing how the religious pluralist movement has its roots in a far greater whole, a crisis of civilization. But on the other hand, precisely on account of these developments, the value judgments that we can and must pass on the phenomenon of pluralism in the name of Christian authenticity can be more selective and clearer.

It is fashionable today to formulate, right at the beginning of an exposition, a working hypothesis, a guiding idea. I will therefore say at once that it is all the easier to understand and practice Christian pluralism the more it is set in the framework of the Christian plan of divinization and humanization. To the extent to which Christians live by grace and the Revelation of Christ, they are assumed into the unity of the Christian mystery and united in charity (Col. 4, 1 ff.). Their diversity in human groups and their individuality as human persons nominally loved by God (Gal. 2, 20) are not suppressed, however, for "grace does not suppress nature" or, if a richer formula is desired, "the divine does not suppress the human," it gives it its whole meaning, it purifies it and perfects it. A plurality of persons and groups compatible with unity in Christ will not be threatened, therefore, by it. The only plurality that will not be Christian will be that of the group that withdraws into itself, persons who refuse *koinonia* and who thereby reject the demands of human dignity just as much as the demands of divinization[6].

2. The Church is both "one" and "catholic"

A) 20th century man torn between "planetization" and "isolation."

If we try to relate the problem of religious pluralism to the great movements of thought today, we must consider in the first place, that now, towards the end of the 20th century, men are more and more unified and, at the same time, seek to save a certain autonomy which seems to them to be the very condition of their identity. *Gaudium et Spes* (n. 6) had already made the following remark, in this direction: ". . . a man's ties with his fellows are constantly being multiplied. At the same time 'socialization' brings further ties, without, however, always promoting appropriate personal development and truly personal relationships ("personalization")."

Sociologists in the last few years do not differ in their conclusions. With MacLuhan, they have realized that the world has become "one planetary village",[7] in which all men and all women live more or less in the same way. There are still differences, it is true—alas cruel ones—between the first, the second and the third world, but they tend to become less distinct. There cannot be an earthquake thousands of miles away, there cannot be a drought in distant countries without our being informed of it within six hours. Newspapers and TV put before our eyes tragic photos of starving or abandoned children, to give us a psychological shock and create an impulse of solidarity. Within each of the "worlds," in Europe, for example, people drive the same cars, read the same books and see the same films. We are rightly proud of these similarities, which tone down local differences.

However, if man today has the impression he is a citizen of a "planetary village," he also feels, on the other hand, that he is isolated, that he has become a being without roots and without solidarity. The old groups of the past are dissolving: the "patriarchal family" is tending to give way to the molecular family composed of father, mother and child, without the grandparents, uncles, aunts and cousins. Nationalism is dying out and many young people feel uneasy in the presence of anything reminiscent of the fatherland; from one point of view their reserve with regard to military service can be explained in this way. The professions are becoming international: doctors working in research and engineers can be utilized in foreign countries by multinational companies in whose eyes they are interchangeable. So there comes into play a defense mechanism, "regionalization." Abroad, people pay particular attention to their fellow countrymen and, with them, they try to keep their identity, in order not to be completely assimilated. At home, they stress regionalization: in nearly all the West European countries which have united in the Common Market and which are playing very loyally the card of economic and cultural expansion, there are, on the other hand, local or regional movements. In Italy, in France, in Belgium, the "regions" are taking on new importance.

In short, one would think that, taking for granted an inevitable rapprochement in ever larger groups, men today are taking out a reinsurance policy in the opposite direction by stressing local differences, and cultural and ideological pluralism.

B) Equilibrium of unity and diversity in the Church of Vatican II

In the Church, this twofold play of centripedal and centrifugal forces is manifested in the same way. The Church has desired to come into closer contact with the different civilizations as well as with other Christian denominations, with all religions as well as with the "world" itself. The result was a movement of differentiation and pluralism which, in the spirit of Vatican II which promoted it under the guidance of John XXIII and Paul VI, was in perfect agreement with the unity of the Church and her necessary role for salvation.[8] In the whole of history, Vatican II certainly represented—at least on the plane of intention—a particularly happy moment of equilibrium in the consciousness of a Church which is both "one" and "catholic," that is, adequately present to all peoples, to their particularities, to their desire to be themselves.

"The chosen People of God is one: 'one Lord, one faith, one baptism'," recalls *Lumen Gentium* (n. 32) in accordance with Ephesians 4, 5. Factors of unity are at once put forward: "As members, they share a common dignity from their rebirth in Christ. They have the same filial grace and the same vocation to perfection. They possess in common one salvation,[9] one hope, and one undivided charity." As the visible sign and guarantor of this unity, Vatican II, referring explicitly to Vatican I, recalls the special role of Peter, the head of the apostolic college as the Pope is the head of the episcopal body. "Christ placed blessed Peter over the other apostles, and instituted in him a permanent and visible source and foundation of unity of faith and fellowship" (*Lumen Gentium,* n. 18).

But on the other hand the Church recognized unreservedly and without any difficulty the diversity of cultures and the protection due to them (*Gaudium et Spes,* n. 56). In the name of the ties between faith and cultures, the Council declares: "Faithful to her own tradition and at the same time conscious of her universal mission, she (the Church) can enter into communion with various cultural modes, to her own enrichment and theirs too" (*Gaudium et Spes,* n. 58, 4). "Living in various circumstances during the course of time, the Church, too, has used in her preaching the discoveries of different cultures to spread and explain the message of Christ to all nations, to probe it and more deeply understand it, and to give it better expression in liturgical celebrations and in the life of the diversified community of the faithful" (*Gaudium et Spes,* n. 58, 2). The decree *Ad Gentes* (n. 22) devotes a special section to "Diversity in Unity," where we read in particular:

"The seed which is the Word of God sprouts from the good ground watered by divine dew. From this ground the seed draws nourishing elements which it transforms and assimilates into itself. Finally it bears much fruit. Thus, in imitation of the plan of the Incarnation, the young Churches, rooted in Christ and built up on the foundation of the apostles, take to themselves in a wonderful exchange all the riches of the nations which were given to Christ as an inheritance. From the customs and traditions of their people, from their wisdom and their learning, from their arts and sciences, these Churches borrow all those things which can contribute to the glory of their Creator, the revelation of the Saviour's grace, or the proper arrangement of Christian life." Here we are given as an example the same faith in Christian Revelation, explained by the Magisterium, which according to St. Anselm's formula, "seeks for understanding" (*fidem quaerens intellectum)* taking into account the "philosophy and wisdom of these peoples" in such a way that errors will be eliminated while the presentation will be adapted. "Thanks to such a procedure, every appearance of syncretism and of false particularism can be excluded, and Christian life can be accommodated to the genius and the dispositions of each culture" *(Ad Gentes,* n. 22).

ONE SOLE REALITY

C) Imbalance of radical pluralism

We may well wonder whether, ten years after the Council, this equilibrium still exists, at least among a noisy minority, which must not, however, cast doubts on the faithfulness of the vast majority of Catholics to Christ (10). For this noisy, active minority, three essential Christian ideas are questioned, so that a real "crisis of identity" arises.

In the first place "they will not recognize in the Church one sole reality, the result of a dual human and divine element, similar to the mystery of the Word Incarnate, which makes her a "community of faith, hope and charity on earth, a visible whole," by means of which Christ spreads truth and grace for everyone. Consequently they oppose the Hierarchy, as if any act of opposition of this kind were a constituent moment of the truth about the Church, which was to be discovered such as Christ had established her."[11] In such a perspective, contestation is sought as a means of saving the individual or small group from an authority which is declared *a priori* to be oppressive. Thus we arrive at the radical pluralism of "quot capita, tot sententiae." Little groups, small theological circles, claim for themselves the authority they have denied to the hierarchical Church.

If this guarantee of doctrinal unity has been swept away, it is easy to see that two other essential Christian ideas are questioned: Revelation, and salvation by Christ. Revelation is no longer the manifestation of Christ bringing men truth and making them participate in divine nature (*Dei Verbum,* n. 2). It is only, according to a famous Protestant exegete, awareness of what man needs to be better as a man. Consequently the Christian plan could be summed up in a very general directive, on the transcendental plane, "be a man," and all doctrine or categorical precept would have to be borrowed from human sciences.

It is quite certain that the new human sciences can render the faith great services as Platonism and Aristotelianism did in the past. But the Fathers who utilized these philosophical doctrines did not think for a moment of putting them in the place of Christian Revelation. Today, on the contrary, some people do not hesitate to look elsewhere than in God's Word preserved in the tradition of the Church for a doctrine to believe and to live. They claim a pluralism that breaks with everything, for they set up against the Faith of Tradition a view of man and a plan of liberation that no longer have anything in common with the Gospel. For example, some people will doubt the Resurrection of Christ and will say that the real meaning of this belief is the new lease of energy the Apostles, left alone, drew from the realization that they must continue Jesus' work. Then, too, Christ will be presented as "such an extraordinary man that he can be called divine," but there will be no question of recognizing the eternal Word in Him.

If some Christians destroy the faith in this way and yet wish to remain in the Church in the name of a radical pluralism, how can we doubt the danger of the pluralism that is the basis of the theory of the "anonymous Christian" extolled by others? If we wish to see Christians unbeknown to themselves in all men of goodwill, in whom grace is at work, we simply recognize with Vatican II the truth of the *semina Verbi* scattered in the world (*Ad Gentes,* n. 11 and 15) and the importance of *preparatio evangelica (Lumen Gentium,* n. 16). But there is a great difference between the appeal that Christ makes to all to call them to his kingdom, on the one hand, and the completion of this work in acceptance of the Gospel and faithfulness to grace, on the other hand. Now, some supporters of the theory of the "anonymous Christian" pay no heed to it so that for them faith, adherence to the Church, sacramental and liturgical life are unimportant. Provided a man be "of goodwill," he is a Christian without knowing it; it is useless to trouble him by preaching the Gospel to him with its demands regarding thought and life.

As can be seen, this conception of extreme pluralism, according to the penetrating analysis of H. Urs von Balthasar[12] "gives rise . . . to the impression that the visible Church is only an institution with a multitude of rules, laws and regulations indicating what we must believe and how we must live, while the living substance of this institution might just as well be scattered outside it in the world. . . . If the real substance of Christianity is scattered among the whole of humanity, the only thing that remains to distinguish 'the Church of Christ' is the form, the skeleton." Pluralism understood in this perspective is likely to be a pretext for no longer belonging to the visible Church or for carrying out "opposition from inside," as was said above.

3. Truth: communion of the subject and the object

A) Opening on the real

The problem of pluralism does not just lead us to study the reactions of 20th century man in search of his identity, which he runs the risk of putting in the wrong place. It also obliges us to study his "art of thinking." In religious, philosophical and scientific knowledge, there is always more or less a twofold pole: the object known and the subject knowing. Classical philosophy defines truth as *"adequatio rei et intellectus"*; it tries to open the way to truth by having recourse to intuition, induction, and deduction, the rules of which vary according to the different disciplines. Thus, we "know what is," we "know what must be done." In history, for example, the task of criticism is not to demolish, as some people have said rather hastily, but an investigation, an attempt to examine documents and testimonies in order to try to see the event as completely as possible.

In this mentality, trust in the specialist, the "master," the expert, was not considered an abdication but the means of obtaining through someone else a conviction at which one could not completely arrive by oneself. In the field of morality, recourse to a revelation or to reason (according to whether it is theology or natural ethics) was the fundamental method, completed by trust in authors whose opinions made it possible to find practical directives. Under these conditions, as can be seen, not all pluralism was excluded, for the researches of each person as well as his trust in different masters could lead to various formulations and to one or other different conclusion. There remained, however, a vast common foundation and a historical constant, and above all the conviction that it was possible to arrive at the truth.

PRINCIPLE OF REALISM

B) Hypertrophy of the Subject

The Truth! Certain contemporaries find it hard to admit such a claim. They are led by the "masters of suspicion," and to those who speak to them of truth, they like to reply as Pilate did to Jesus, when He said He had come to the world to bear witness to truth: *"Quid est veritas?"* (Jn. 18, 38).

Hegel implanted in the modern world the conviction that truth follows certain stages of development, thesis, antithesis and synthesis. Nietzsche spoke of the creation of values by the different societies in the sense that they attach very great importance to the goods which they lack or for which they long. John Stuart Mill defended the thesis that it is vain to seek the truth and that we must be content with what is useful. Hence the contempt for rational justifications and the search for practical attitudes that can be linked up with very different systems. Orthopraxis, that is, effective and humanitarian action, adapts itself to the most radical pluralism as regards theoretical opinion, that is, it cares nothing about orthodoxy as it cares nothing about philosophical truth.

A certain sociology has taken over, claiming that all doctrines were conditioned by the environments that formulated them, even without their authors knowing it. Since the world has changed, since the fascination of certain researches holds out prospects of a new type of man, one would indeed be wrong not to admit relativism, the new form of the eternal temptation of scepticism. Marcuse who is the master of the cultural revolution of the years 1968-1970 wrecks "the principle of realism," which his master Freud had kept to counterbalance the "principle of pleasure."

Among some of those who mould opinion, the idea of objectivity is sometimes questioned. The attempt is no longer made to reach the facts but to describe personal reactions. Sociological research—so useful in itself for those who wish to know states of minds—threatens to take the place of doctrinal and critical judgment. As can be seen, in all these tendencies we find the same hypertrophy of the Ego, of the subject. It is no longer a question of seeking or even esteeming the unity of truth but of recognizing and justifying differences of opinion among groups. A subsequent stage consists in demanding freedom for all opinions and all ways of acting, in the name of pluralism. Let us say incidentally that it will not be possible to overcome the present crisis of scepticism without a philosophical effort in the direction of realism and objectivity.

C) The I of the Christian and the divine You

It would be vain to hope that the faithful of today will completely escape the present scepticism. All the more so in that the latter is connected with an eternal heaviness, a resistance that man always puts up against divine truth. Called by his God, the Creator and Redeemer, man has always been tempted to retire within himself, to think what he wished and not what was—*a fortiori* "the One who is"—to will what he desired and not what he should do.

This is the underlying meaning of the story of Genesis, which starts with the break with God and ends with aggressiveness against other men, whether it is a question of Cain killing Abel or the dispersion of the peoples at Babel. But God would not be defeated and he always recalled his people to monotheistic faith and brotherhood. In his Son, this story and this work of salvation was extended to all peoples, to whom grace and truth are brought: *"gratia et veritas per Iesum Christum facta est"* (Jn. 1, 17). Christ calls his apostles and through them, all those to whom they are sent, bringing them more life, light and charity than is in them. The religious "subject" does not disappear, for he must personally commit himself through real faith, hope and charity, but he has recourse, like all his brothers, to one mediator only: *Unus enim Deus, unus et mediator Dei et hominum, homo Christus Jesus qui dedit redemptionem semetipsum pro omnibus* (1 Tim. 2, 5-6).

Here unity is saved in God without, however, neglecting the subject's own characteristics, without ignoring the diversity of vocations, ministries and gifts as the Apostle of the Gentiles declares in 1 Cor. 12, 1 ff. Not all pluralism, therefore, is ruled out; it could even be said that it is necessary; "Si totum corpus oculus, ubi auditus? Si totum auditus, ubi odoratus" (1 Cor. 12, 17).

It will not be the same if it is sought to replace the pluralism based on the objectivity of the Faith to be believed and applied in life, with a pluralism in which everyone re-invents his faith and his morality more or less subjectively. It was this danger, a strangely contemporary one, that was pointed out in *Paterna cum benevolentia:* (n. 4): "What are we to say of a pluralism that considers faith and its expression not as a common and therefore ecclesial heritage but as *an individual rediscovery* of free criticism and free examination of God's word? In fact, without the mediation of the Magisterium of the Church to which the Apostles entrusted thier own magisterium and which, consequently, teaches only 'what was transmitted,' secure union with Christ through the Apostles, namely, 'those who transmit what they have themselves received,' is compromised. For this reason once perseverance in the doctrine transmitted by the Apostles is compromised it happens that, wishing, perhaps, to elude the difficulties of the mystery, formulas of illusory comprehensibility are sought which dissolve its real content; in this way *doctrines are constructed which do not adhere to the objectivity of the faith* or which are even contrary to it, and furthermore contain elements that contradict one another."

4. Plurality of pluralism

A) Pluralism of cohesion and pluralism of division

If an impression emerges from what we have just said, it is that the term "pluralism" must be understood in several meanings and that it is applied to very different fields, for which the value judgments must also be different. In the first place, it is necessary to stress the essential difference between a pluralism of concord or diversity and a pluralism of division and dissent. These terms appear in the Apostolic Exhortation *Paterna cum benevolentia* of December 8, 1974, not, certainly, as technical expressions, which would be out of place in this kind of document, but as very enlightening reference marks which theological work can and must utilize. I will quote only paragraph 4 of point VI: "The fact remains, however, that in the structure of the body of Christ there is a diversity of members and offices, and that this diversity leads to inevitable tensions. They can be met with even in the Saints, but not such as to kill concord . . . to destroy charity. How can we prevent them from degenerating into division? It is from that very diversity of persons and functions that the firm principle of ecclesial cohesion is derived."

It is easy to see in what these two attitudes differ. The pluralism that stresses diversities in the life of the Church and Christians, remains persuaded that Christian Revelation is the same for all and in all ages because it is centered on Christ: *Christus heri et hodie: ipse et in saecula* (Heb. 13, 8). It finds in the Magisterium and pontifical authority a guarantee of the legitimacy of the pastoral adaptations which take into account the faith, morality and sacramental life common to all Christians (Mt. 28, 18-20). That is why some people think that though the term "pluralism" was widely used from 1965 to 1970, when it was not yet ambiguous, it would now be better to use it less, with all the clarifications that are necessary, and to return more often to the language of "diversity" and "particularity" used by the Council.[13]

ESSENTIAL DISTINCTION

The term "pluralism," in fact, is now taken by some people, as often as not, in the meaning of *dissent*. The essential difference depends on the fact that the necessary unity in Christ, under the authority of the Hierarchy and the Magisterium, has disappeared, as can be seen from the following observations in *Paterna cum benevolentia:* "The process we have described (the obscuring of the role of the Church) takes on the form of a doctrinal dissent which claims to be sponsored by theological pluralism and which is not infrequently carried to the point of dogmatic relativism. . . . The internal oppositions affecting the different sectors of ecclesial life, if they are stabilized in a state of dissent, lead to setting up against the one institution and community of salvation, a plurality of institutions or communities of dissent which are not in conformity with the nature of the Church."[14] Already in 1971 Paul VI had asked the question: "Where is it headed, a certain indiscriminate doctrinal pluralism, arbitrary and centrifugal?"[15]

Starting from this essential distinction, it can quite easily be seen how the problem of pluralism is raised in the different sectors of the life of Church. A certain liturgical pluralism probably existed from the very first generation, for while the communities of Jerusalem, Rome, Antioch and Corinth certainly wished to relive the Lord's Supper round the Apostles or their representatives, they did so in different languages and in different cultural environments which led to the difference of rites between East and West with a whole series of diversifications. We have perhaps forgotten this because, in the West, we are emerging from a time of fixity and uniformity.

But on the other hand we must not lose sight, under the pretext of creativeness and diversity, of the fact that there is a unitary structure of the Blessed Sacrament and that we cannot disregard the forms which the apostolic and postapostolic generations gave it and which survive in the different rites. The Protestants themselves have kept numerous elements! Finally, ten years of creativeness have shown us that the faithful themselves do not appreciate change for the sake of change, diversity from one Sunday to another and from one parish to another. People always forget to speak of the "sensus fidelium" in this connection! Moreover, it is not in the field of the liturgy that the great difficulties of diversification are raised today.[16] They occur at the level of faith and theology, ecclesiology and culture. Let us study them in the aspect they have assumed recently.

B) The problem of pluralism on the theological plane

Two recent declarations of Paul VI (the Apostolic Exhortation of December 8, the closing Address of the Synod, on October 26, 1974), sum up well the official doctrine of the Magisterium in this connection. The Sovereign Pontiff recognizes the legitimacy of a pluralism of concord in theological research and in a more and more thorough investigation of the Christian mystery on condition that the unity of revealed datum, such as it was and is formulated by the Magisterium, be saved. On the other hand, he rejects a pluralism of dissent in the exposition of the Christian doctrine (theology in the widest sense) carried out by those who set themselves up as an anti-magisterium. Let us take a closer look at this.

The pluralism of concord is manifested in research work, which is evidently marked by the culture and personal characteristics of those who undertake it. In connection with this pluralism, the Pope declares: "We recognize pluralism of research and thought, which explores and expounds dogma in different ways, but without eliminating its identical objective meaning, as having legitimate citizenship in the Church, as a natural component of catholicity, and a sign of cultural riches and of personal commitment on the part of those who belong to her."[17]

In the last few years, the Sovereign Pontiff has often recalled the definitive character of "the doctrine sanctioned by pontifical and conciliar definitions,"[18] the "permanent up-to-dateness" of the Councils, and he specially mentioned Nicaea (325), Constantinople (381), Ephesus (431), Chalcedon (451),[19] Trent (1563), Vatican I (1871).[20] But that does not mean that Christian thought has ground to a standstill and that, while taking into account what is definitively acquired, it is not possible to find presentations better suited to new cultures. It is in this sense that *Paterna cum benevolentia* sees a legitimate manifestation of pluralism of concord: "We admit, in fact," the Holy Father Paul VI continues, "that a balanced theological pluralism finds its foundation in the very mystery of Christ, the unfathomable riches of which (cf. Eph. 3, 8) go beyond the capacities of expression of all ages and all cultures. The doctrine of the faith, which is necessarily derived from this mystery —since, with regard to salvation, 'God's mystery is nothing but Christ' —calls for ever new investigations. As a matter of fact, the perspectives of the Word of God are so numerous, and the perspectives of the faithful who study it are so numerous, that convergence in the same faith is never exempt from personal particularities in the adherence of each one. However, the different stresses laid in the understanding of the same faith do not prejudice its essential content, for the latter finds its unity in common adherence to the Magisterium of the Church. This same magisterium, as the proximate norm, determines the faith of all, and at the same time guarantees everyone against the subjective judgment of all divergent interpretations of the faith."[21]

It is not a question, therefore, of blocking research or imposing undue uniformity: each theologian, in communion with the culture of his time and his people, has the mission of exploring further the unfathomable mysteries of Christ and of setting them forth in a way that is more and more adapted to the different cultures. But this effort must not deform the message of Christ himself and transform it in such a way that theologians arrive at pluralism of dissent. This was the danger that the Sovereign Pontiff pointed out at the end of the synod. Speaking of "the necessity of finding a better expression of faith, corresponding to the racial, social and cultural environment," Paul VI added: "This is, certainly, a prerequisite for the authenticity and efficacy of evangelization. It would be dangerous, however, to speak of theologies diversified according to continents and cultures. The content of faith is either Catholic or it is not. All of us, moreover, have received the faith from an uninterrupted and constant tradition: Peter and Paul did not disguise it to adapt it to the ancient Jewish, Greek or Roman world, but they watched over its authenticity, over the truth of the one message, presented in the diversity of languages (Acts. 2, 8)." [23]

Likewise unity based on Revelation and its authentic presentation by the Magisterium is endangered when certain theologians claim to submit the decisions of the Hierarchy to their own favorable "reception"[24] or openly take up positions against them in the name of a theological pluralism of dissent which pretends to be a valid criterion, a "theological place" *(locus theologicus).*[25]

UNITY ENDANGERED

C) Pluralism and ecclesiology

There has always been a certain ecclesial pluralism, for from the first generations the Judeo-Christian communities had features that distinguished them from the Hellenistic communities. At the present time, churches of Latin rite and Catholic churches of Oriental rite show differences in liturgy and canon law. Vatican II reaffirmed the legitimacy of a certain pluralism in these fields, but always in conformity with the directives that have been and may be given by the competent ecclesiastical authority. St. Paul spoke of the Church of the Thessalonians (1 Th. 1, 1 and 2 Th. 1, 1), of the Churches of Galatia (Gal. 1, 2), the Church of God at Corinth (1 Cor. 1, 2). But "the Church" also appears as one and universal; the word is used in the singular to indicate the group of local Churches established among the Jews and among the Gentiles. "This term Church in the universal sense," Mons. Cerfaux wrote ". . . has its roots in the past and looks towards the future. It recalls 'The Church of God' of the early community, and is thus linked up with the very first community of the Church (the Messianic assembly symbolized in the desert Church), which St. Paul spoke of in his first epistle to the Corinthians. It looks towards the future, detaching the Christian people more from its local contingencies and promising a more marked idealization, as happened for the heavenly Jersualem or the community of the Saints in the Apocalypse."[26]

The awareness of unity has been asserted more and more in episcopal collegiality, in the ecumenical Councils but above all around the primacy of the Bishop of Rome. It was at these ecumenical Councils, at Nicaea and at Trent, that the Church strengthened her unity against the divisions which, alas, occurred.

Two dangers appear in this connection today. The stress on local particularisms, on the "little communities," on the demands of the

Spirit, said to be opposed to structures, threatens to cause us to lose sight of the unity of the *koinonia.* That is why Paul VI, in his address concluding the Synod, recalled that the Lord entrusted to the successor of Peter "the important, perennial, loving office of feeding his lambs and ewes, of strengthening his brethren, of being the foundation and sign of Church unity. His intervention, therefore, cannot be reduced merely to extraordinary circumstances. No: we say so trembling because of the responsibility that devolves upon us: he is and remains the ordinary Pastor of the whole flock." Going on to recall the words of *Lumen Gentium,* n. 22, 2, the Pope adds: "It is not a dialectic of powers that is at stake here: it is a question of a single desire, to correspond to God's will, with complete love, each with the contribution of the faithful accomplishment of his own office." [27]

A second danger of false ecclesial pluralism is found at the level of non-Catholic ecumenism. In the last two or three years, this false ecumenism has considered that Christ's true Church is made up of the federation of the different Christian denominations which are all put on the same footing. Taking as a pretext certain expressions of Vatican II, which have been misinterpreted, these Christian denominations are said to have ministries that are in practice as valid as the apostolic structures of the traditional ministry: episcopate, priesthood, diaconate. It has even been said that the infallibility of the Church could not be realized without the agreement of the communities of the 16th century Reformation. It is attempts of this kind which undermine from the inside the credibility of the Church of Christ[28] and question its unique and universal role, contrast the community of the disciples of Jesus with the present-day Church and contest the authority of Pastors. Referring once more to Vatican II, Paul VI reaffirms that "this Church, constituted and organized in the world as a society, subsists in the Catholic Church, which is governed by the successor of Peter and by the bishops in union with that successor, although many elements of sanctification and of truth can be found outside of her visible structure" (*Lumen Gentium,* n. 8).[29]

D) Pluralism and culture

Cultural pluralism is perhaps the one that concerns most Christians today. And yet, in principle, it could be said that the cultural sector is the one in which Christian pluralism is most at ease. Everything that is human is ours: these words of Terence were repeated by Paul VI in his famous address on pluralism delivered on May 14, 1969. Divine grace assumes human nature in all its geographical diversity and in all its historical dimensions. Then, too, even if there is a constant exchange between faith and the various cultures (*Gaudium et Spes,* n. 42, 43, 44), we are here in the field of the "rightful autonomy of earthly affairs" (*Gaudium et Spes,* n. 36) and of the distinction between faith and reason (*Gaudium et Spes,* n. 59).

YOUNG CHURCHES

When we examine this problem concretely, however, as was often done at the 1974 Synod, we realize that it raises great difficulties. In spite of the great efforts made in the last few years, concurrently with the irreversible movement of decolonization, one gets the impression that the young churches of the Third World feel the need to stress their independence with regard to the Western cultures which, willy-nilly, the first evangelizers brought with them. Whereas in the West cultural movements often take the form of a break with the past, the claims of the Third World (as *Gaudium et Spes,* n. 56 had already noted with an intuition to which not enough attention has been given, perhaps) are formulated in continuity with an "ancestral wisdom" which they feel is threatened. Hence the demand for an "authenticity" which seems legitimate in itself even if some people are tempted to speak of ingratitude.

The new Christian communities, faced with faithfulness both to the authenticity of their ancestral traditions and to the identity and singularity of Christianity, are reliving the great hours experienced by early Christianity when it came into contact with Greek and Latin cultures in the 2nd century. The key to this work of adaptation is contained in a few instructions, also indicated by *Gaudium et Spes* (n. 58): "to enter into communion with various cultural modes, make fruitful, as it were from within, the spiritual qualities and gifts of every people and every age" but also "to combat and remove the errors and evils resulting from sinful allurements." It is necessary, in fact, to beware of a twofold exaggeration. Formerly the colonizing peoples often treated with supreme and paternalistic contempt the cultural values of the peoples in tutelage, or more exactly they often ignored them with astonishing ingenuousness. Today when these values are again put forward and when the traces of westernization are disappearing, one after the other, we must keep our heads and not consider all ancestral traditions positive and acceptable. The most obvious example that comes to mind, and which was mentioned several times at the Synod, is polygamy.

EXCLUSIVE PRIVILEGE

But here again, the young churches are merely repeating the process lived in the past by the churches of the Mediterranean world. Mention is often made of the remarks of apologists such as Tertullian and the author of *The Letter to Diognetus* which show the desire of their co-religionists not to conform with Jewish segregation in order to accept fully the ways of life of their environment, in politics, in social relations and in commerce. But it is forgotten, perhaps, that at the same time these Christians were aware of and full of wonder at, the specificity of the Christian vocation and the divine and human riches that Christ had offered them, not as an exclusive privilege but to be given to everyone. They know very well that their Christian vocation prevented them from accepting all the customs of their environment. Thus they undertook, for example, a campaign to arouse public opinion against infanticide and abortion.[30]

Ontologically, in Christ, perfectly God and perfectly man, the divine and the human harmonize. In Christians, who know they are under "the perpetual threat" of sin (GS, n. 58, 4), on the psychological plane, the human sometimes appears as an obstacle to divinization which grace and asceticism must overcome. But this effort does not aim at destroying the human, it seeks to "perfect and restore (it) in Christ" according to the expression of Ephesians 1, 10, repeated by *Gaudium et Spes*, n. 58, 4. It is the same for the different aspects of the various cultures. Those which cannot be reconciled with Christ will be abandoned with more or less regret. Cultural pluralism will seem to suffer as a result but actually it will survive in a purified form and will find a new meaning in the Lord and in the men who live by Him.

NOTES

[1] See in this connection the *Vocabulaire technique de la philosophie* by Lalande and F. J. Thonnard, *Précis d'histoire de la philosophie*, fifth edition, Tournai, 1966, p. 528, note 1. For the different meanings today, documentation will be found in *Le pluralisme, histoire, sociologie, philosophie*, 1972 Symposium in Montreal, published by the Fides publishing house of that city in 1974.

[2] Vatican II spoke twice of pluralism, on the plane of civil society only, to combat a monopoly of schools that would destroy the freedom of Christian teaching: . . . "Excluso scholarum monopolio, quod nativis humanae personae iuribus . . . pacificae civium consortioni necnon pluralismo in permultis societatibus hodie vigenti adversatur" (*Gravissimum Educationis*, n. 6). In n. 7, the term occurs again in connection with civil societies that recognize the legitimate freedom of parents in the exercise of the duty of bringing up their children, "pluralismi hodiernae societatis ratione habita et debitae libertati religiosae consulentes."

[3] This author, who claims a faith without a dogma, wrote recently (Signal, December 18, 1974): "Today there is no longer ONE Church, ONE interpretation of the dogmas, but different churches, the message which crystallizes round the person of Christ."

[4] In his Apostolic Exhortation *Paterna cum benevolentia* of December 8, 1974, the Holy Father pointed out precisely that the dialectics of unity and diversity lived in the Church can be compared "to the similar situation in which civil society is living today. . . . Unfortunately, the Holy Father writes, the Church seems to be suffering a little from the backlash of these circumstances; but she must not assimilate what is rather a pathological state."

[5] These works and the book based on them were directed by Prof. J. Ratzinger: *Internationale Theologen-Kommission, Die Einheit des Glaubens und der theologische Pluralismus*, Einsiedeln, Johannes Verlag, 1973. An Italian translation has appeared; Spanish, French and English editions are being prepared.

[6] The connection between the community of men in grace and their natural solidarity in society and respect, was stressed by *Gaudium et Spes*, n. 41 and n. 42.

[7] Marshall MacLuhan and Quentin Fiore, *Guerre et paix dans le village planetaire*, Paris, 1973.

[8] I will not go into a technical discussion here and I refer readers for further information to the work, still so valuable, of the late Mons. G. Phillips, *L'Eglise et son mystère au deuxième Concile du Vatican. Histoire, texte et commentaire de la Constitution Lumen Gentium*, Tournai, Desclee, 2 vols., 1967-68.

[9] The necessity of the Church as the sacrament of salvation, offered to everyone, is very clearly recalled in n. 14 of *Lumen Gentium*.

[10] *Paterna cum benevolentia* (n. 3) emphasizes the contrast between "the vast majority of the faithful" and "the ferments of unfaithfulness to the Holy Spirit which are found here and there in the Church today and which are trying, alas, to undermine it from inside. The promoters and victims of this process" are "actually not numerous. . . ."

[11] *Paterna cum benevolentia,* n. 3.

[12] Hans Urs von Balthasar, *Dans l'engagement de Dieu, Paris,* 1973, p. 8-9.

[13] In the Vatican II text, alongside the pluralism of civil society mentioned above, the terms used when it is a question of the Church are rather *diversitas, varietas, multiplicitas, particularitas, peculiaritas.* Fr. de Lubac has recommended on several occasions a return to the vocabulary of the Council.

[14] *Paterna cum benevolentia,* n. 4.

[15] General audience July 21, 1971.

[16] In the above-mentioned volume (n. 5) of the International Theological Commission there are numerous texts of the holy Father in favor of a pluralism of cohesion in the field of the liturgy, ecclesiastical discipline and spirituality. They are summed up in the following sentence from *Paterna cum benevolentia,* n. 4: "We also recognize the inestimable values that it (pluralism of cohesion) introduces in the field of Christian spirituality, ecclesial and religious institutions, as well as in the field of liturigcal expressions and disciplinary norms: values which are found in this 'variety of local churches with one common aspiration (which) is particularly splendid evidence of the catholicity of the undivided Church' " (*Lumen Gentium,* n. 23).

[17] *Paterna cum benevolentia,* n. 4.

[18] *Address to the Sacred College,* December 23, 1972.

[19] *Address after the Journey to Turkey,* August 2, 1967.

[20] *Address for the Centenary of the First Vatican Council,* December 8, 1969.

[21] *Paterna cum benevolentia,* n. 4.

[22] *Paterna cum benevolentia,* n. 4.

[23] *Closing Address of the Synod,* October 28, 1974.

[24] *Paterna cum benevolentia,* n. 6.

[25] *Paterna cum benevolentia,* n. 4: "This pluralism is sometimes considered as a legitimate *locus theologicus,* so as to permit the taking up of positions against the authentic Magisterium of the Roman Pontiff himself and the episcopal hierarchy, the only authoritative interpreters of the divine revelation contained in Sacred Tradition and in the Holy Scriptures.

[26] L. Cerfaux, *La théologie de l'Eglise suivant saint Paul,* Paris, 1965, page 253.

[27] *Address on October 26, 1974.*

[28] *Paterna cum benevolentia,* n. 3.

[29] *Paterna cum benevolentia,* n. 3.

[30] *S. Congregatio pro Doctrina Fidei, Declaratio de Abortu procurato,* 1974, notae 6, 7, 8, 9.

IDEOLOGY AND PRAXIS: FAITH AND MORALITY

by Antonio M. Javierre, S.D.B.

PROFESSOR OF DOGMATIC THEOLOGY AT THE PONTIFICAL SALESIAN UNIVERSITY

1. Introduction

1. The profession of prophet is certainly no easy one. Criticism does not forgive mistakes in calculation, whatever may be the merits of the prediction.

Charges have now been brought against a large number of prophets. They had been convincing us for years that ideologies were about to disappear. The diagnosis seemed faultless, the disease incurable, collapse immediate. It had even become fashionable to refer to the downfall of ideologies.

Yet, despite the forecasts, ideologies live on and, it seems, with increased vitality. The number of pseudo-prophets has therefore increased. Their biggest mistake, perhaps, was to have ignored aspects of the phenomenon which are so mysterious as to make it downright paradoxical.

2. It is not easy to imagine the energy potential latent in a serene definition such as Prini's: "Ideology is a conceptual apparatus which expresses, interprets and justifies the collective needs and aspirations of a group, for the purposes of setting up and maintaining or modifying a certain system of relationships (economic, social and political) both among the members of the group itself and between the latter and other groups."

The subject, present right from the beginning at the very heart of Marxism, shows conceptual variations which make analysis a baffling matter. On the one side there is Marx's firm condemnation of ideology put in the service of the interests of the ruling class; which does not prevent him, on the other hand, from having recourse to ideology to describe precisely the goals to be reached in the long march towards liberation.

BEYOND FRONTIERS

Ideology, yes or no? The ambivalence of the term complicates its relationships. Critics seemed unanimous in excluding dialogue from its horizon; "and this—as Pareyson explains—because ideologies are by their very nature totalistic, that is, they claim to be a complete and total view of the world." But once more the facts belie the logical forecasts: the recent structures of the World Council of Churches have set up a group for the animation of dialogue beyond denominational frontiers, including among the new interlocutors non-Christian religions and "ideologies of our times."

The anathemas of "German Ideology" "against morality, religion, metaphysics and all the other ideologies did not foreshadow this friendly meeting of religions and Marxism. It remains to be seen to what extent Pareyson's diagnosis is objective; because dialogue is something more than taking part in a round table in a gesture of goodwill.

3. The paradox involves the Catholic world even more strikingly.

There was the widespread conviction that "Christianity does not and cannot have an ideology of its own; there was even the conciliar norm that priests are "never to put themselves at the service of any ideology or human faction" (*Presbyterorum Ordinis*, No. 6). Yet there are people today who consider the root of the serious tensions in the post-conciliar period as being ideological in character.

I have on my desk two significant testimonies: the first is a heated denunciation of the so-called "new Christianity," whose features are said to be of specifically Marxist origin. The other, a no less incisive and polemical reply, is a counter-accusation rather than a real defense: in the light of the binomial "theory-praxis" it claims to unmask "traditional Catholicism," reduced to a mere backward ideology, which blocks all real progress.

The episode marks the peak point of the paradox. The glaring ambivalence of the term could not be pushed further. Nor could more devious paths have been found for the dialogue. Although they were the last to enter the lists, some Catholic groups are said to have pressed on to such an extent that they now consider the dialogue phase to be over, having finally reached convergence with Marxism. At the same time, however, their progressive detachment from other Catholics has passed from brotherly *koinonia* to formal dialogue, ending up in open ideological struggle.

The related problems are as vast as they are deep. They should be singled out precisely and examined carefully. I will have to limit myself personally to formulating two questions, which claim no more than to show the seriousness of the problems: Is ideology really the ideal ground for constructive reflection on the identity of the Christian? Can the era of dialogue promulgated by Vatican II inside and outside the domestic frontiers, be considered closed?

2. The Problems of Ideology

Apart from any negative valency, the concepts "faith/ideology," "morality/praxis" present analogies admitting of cross comparisons.

1. We are told that "the modern sciences of man, especially the psychology and sociology of knowledge, have stressed the deep connection between theory and praxis, between the conception of reality or a part of it and the vital interests, the ethico-political choices, the human and social projects of men in their concrete historical situation."

Very well. I wonder, however, if Christian theology did not suggest other sources of inspiration to Kierkegaard when he accused Greek intellectualism of ignorance of the "dialectical category of the passage from understanding to acting." I also doubt that, once the rich message of *Dei Verbum* has been assimilated, it will still be indispensable to have recourse to the binomial "theory/praxis" in order to examine thoroughly the correlative "faith/morality."

God's word has a twofold dimension, noetic and vital, stressed by the Council; not with an abstract reference to the Jewish "dabar," but by taking as the central subject Christ "who is the Mediator and at the same time the fullness of all revelation" (*Dei Verbum*, no. 2). The Father's word is, therefore, Christ. A Christ in whom truth and life meet in a personal embrace.

But then, it is insisted, why not pay more heed to the lessons of "orthopraxis," abandoning the monopoly unjustly given to "orthodoxy?"

The permanent actualization of divine revelation would call for a delicate treatment. In any case it is true that the promise regarding the indefectibility of the word covers both the "correct doctrine" and the "right behavior" of the true Church of Christ. It follows, therefore, that it is legitimate to understand the divine word on the basis of ecclesial "orthopraxis" in the same way as the meaning of the Gospel is studied in the light of the "orthodox" teaching of the Councils.

Attention must be paid, however, to the adjective "orthos" which qualifies both the "doxa" and the "praxis"; and to the "charisma veritatis certum" granted for the authentic interpretation of "true" doxa and "true" praxis which does not belong to theologians, because it is reserved exclusively to the hierarchical Magisterium.

Not any "praxis," therefore, is a real theological source (*locus theologicus*). In view, furthermore, of the conflicting evaluations of an authentic praxis, it is necessary to have recourse to the verdict of pastors, whose *diakonia*, by Christ's will, consists precisely in guiding the flock with authenticity . . . even against the dictates, sometimes tempting, of the surrounding ideologies.

2. Illustrious philosophers of the present day, in agreement with the thought of Augustine, maintain that "the transcendence of Christianity over individual cultures and historical eras calls for the separability of what constitutes the sacral eschatological core of its message at least from the categorical and axiological variations that are characteristic of every age or of every sufficiently differentiated cultural type." There is direct opposition to this view today, in the name of the inseparability of theory and praxis. "Knowledge is never neutral"; and it is therefore utopian "to claim a real political neutrality of the church and theology

in the name of the transcendence of God's Word." Before a human and social project there are no other alternatives but *criticism,* which implies a contrary choice, or *acceptance* which can be open or masked behind an alleged abstention.

It is true that metaphysics cannot be put in brackets. That, too, is a metaphysical behavior. However, the fact of recognizing that one is inevitably compromised in philosophy does not entail the inevitable acceptance of a given system. There always remains at least a relative autonomy. Why should it be any different in the social and political field?

There are, it is true, contexts, both conceptual and practical, in which a way out does not seem possible. In a society divided into classes, we are told, either you side with the oppressed against the oppressors, or you make common cause with the latter against the former.

It should be pointed out at this point that the transcendence of evangelical "morality" over human "praxis" is different in quality from the relationship between "theology" and "theodicy." There is not perfect continuity between the two levels of nature and grace in which the binomial "theory/praxis" is considered.

TRUTH OF SALVATION

By virtue of God's inspiring activity, the divine word is embodied in categories that are sometimes rough, imperfect, even questionable from a strictly scientific perspective, without detriment, however, to the perfection of the message. The salvific truth of the Scripture transcends the astronomical, biological and historical theories in which the word of God palpitates in a living form which is for that very reason mysteriously unitarian. At this point the Incarnation has no adequate equivalent in nature. It presents at once a real "compromise" (because also those affirmations of the poor hagiographer are God's word); yet without detriment to its sovereign "neutrality" (because the truth of salvation is not subjected to the limited horizon of chosen theories).

Why not accept a similar situation as regards the word in real life? The Holy Spirit has "dictated" practical behaviors set in theocratic, monarchical and liberal categories; and all this without favoring any of these sociological patterns. St. Paul formulated moral norms in a context of slavery, without compromising in the slightest his message of Christian freedom. What seems impossible to ideological analysis is no longer so in the light of the Incarnation. Christ, and proportionally Christianity, does not just skim over human realities; it really assumes them; but his frightful "kenosis" does not annihilate his transcendent lordship; it is, in fact, in the depth of humiliation that his kingdom reaches its summit: "regnabit a ligno Deus."

RESPECT FOR FAITHFUL

3. Finally, the condition of pastors and theologians is not identical. The former, when confronted with "Politics" with a capital letter—as Don Bosco would say—in which God's interests are at stake, cannot

remain neutral, even at the risk of shedding their blood in martyrdom in bearing witness. In the field, however, of "politics" with a small letter, it is not only a right but even a duty to ensure that neutrality inspired by the Incarnation, above parties. And that for different reasons: in the first place out of respect for the faithful, who have the freedom of self-determination according to tastes, particular aims and environmental circumstances, always without detriment to Christ's imperatives; secondly out of respect for the specific ministry entrusted to the Pastors of the flock.

Pastoral care does, it is true, impose predilection for the oppressed. It is not always easy to pick them out. Not without humor the President of the Central Committee of the World Council of Churches pointed out at Utrecht his personal perplexity: "In the West I am considered to be 'oppressed', because I am an Indian; in India, on the contrary, I am considered an 'oppressor', because of my intellectual task. What is my real identity?" Unfortunately, very often the diagnosis will be extremely easy and certain; but even there, the program of the Church cannot limit itself merely to a social upheaval that reverses the parts of oppressed and oppressors. What is "new" in Christianity goes far beyond this type of change which always remains on the surface, at the level of particular interests; it aspires, on the contrary, to a real surpassing, to be brought about through a change of the soul in charity.

However, even supposing neutrality to be legitimate and the two categories of "politics accepted," everything is not already clear and solved. The problem remains an enormous one, full of responsibility for the one who must lead the flock. It is not difficult to imagine the Pastor's anguish when he is faced in practice with certain border-line cases. Are they to be included among those which compromise the inalienable interests of God and which cannot be passed over in silence? Are they, on the contrary, among those to be left to the responsible choice of the individual faithful?

This explains the dramatic nature of the decisions; it explains the diversity of the choices; it explains, finally, the short-sighted over-simplification of those who reduce everything to class struggle dialectics. The binomial "theory/praxis" is projected also over the Christian world. It is necessary, however, to take into account decisive and robust variables that are completely unknown in any human ideology.

3. Dialogue and Ideology

Personally I am convinced that dialogue keeps its full validity recognized by Paul VI in his first encyclical and subsequently adopted by the various conciliar documents. Certain interested and partial patterns can be said to be out of date; but not that dialogue which sees its model in trinitarian life itself (*Unitatis Redintegratio*, n. 2).

1. *Open to ideologies?*

I would have nothing to object, provided there is a sincere desire for convergence.

I do not think it is superfluous; because beyond certain groups in Italy the general impression in the World Council is that the dialogue with the ideologies, so promising, is still at the beginning of a way that is expected to be long and laborious.

We should not be frightened by contrary reservations, even if they are solid and justified. Experience teaches that even the most rigorous dogmatisms are more elastic in men than in books. And it is men, fortunately, who are the real protagonists. Moreover, we do not know of any formula more respectful of the values of reality and the rights of the subject than that effort of convergence inspired by sincere humility and real charity.

2. *In connection with ideologies?*

The Council itself sometimes combines the two subjects: ideology that complicates problems and dialogue as a way to solution (cf. *Gaudium et Spes,* n. 85).

If the diagnosis that post-conciliar tensions pass through ideology is really correct, there is no other possibility than recourse to the dialogue therapy.

In this connection, I would just recall the following: the topical interest of the problems must not make us lose sight of the hierarchy of our tasks. Adorno himself warns us of this danger: "When religion is accepted for reasons other than its intrinsic truth, it injures itself. If then, positive religions are working with such enthusiasm today in the same area as other public institutions, even trying to surpass them in their own field, this gives us a glimpse of a certain despair which is in a latent state in their own positivity. I am of the opinion that what the world demands with great urgency today, is rather a real redimensioning than an approval that is already met with nearly everywhere, more frequently than is desirable." . . . Dialogue on ideology? Yes, but in so far as it opens the way to real evangelization.

3. *On the basis of ideology?*

At this point I should answer with a decided "No." The methodology of dialogue requires the effort to find a basis, as solid a one as possible. In dialogue with non-believers we must be content with the elements we have in common. In dialogue within the Church, however, also on the basis of the same principle, we do not have the right to repeat literally the discussion opened with those who are not members of our faith. We have far different foundations on which to base the problem. It is the best way of saving time, for the exact evaluation of what separates us in the whole of our *koinonia;* it is also the certain way to ensure efficiency; because we are sure of being able to illuminate ideologies by God's word; but we are not sure of getting back to true revelation through ideologies.

On the plane of methodology, furthermore, a dialogue between Catholics cannot ignore the triad recalled in *Dei Verbum,* n. 10: "It is clear that sacred tradition, sacred Scripture, and the teaching authority of the

Church, in accord with God's most wise design, are so linked and joined together that one cannot stand without the others, and that all together and each in its own way under the action of the one Holy Spirit contribute effectively to the salvation of souls." Will it be possible to start a specifically Catholic dialogue without too frequent multilations, perhaps out of "professional bias," since we are accustomed to having this kind of ideological conversation with non-Catholics?

To open up to real dialogue is a way of carrying out the Lord's commandment regarding reconciliation, so topical in this Holy Year.

We cannot but be impressed by the comment of the Fathers who stress the urgency of suspending the sacrifice and going to one's brother, even if we do not consider ourselves guilty, even if we think his attitude is unjust. It is the opportunity to convince him of our innocence, or to ask his forgiveness for what was unknown to us.

I would like to approach my brothers with this attitude, with the desire, that is, to eliminate any spirit of polemics to which I may unconsciously give rise. Because the God of truth and the Prince of Peace is the same. And then to continue the interrupted sacrifice, which has become unanimous, Catholic.

CATHOLICS' FREEDOM OF OPTION IN PUBLIC LIFE

by Bishop Ramon Torrella Cascante

VICE PRESIDENT OF THE PONTIFICAL COMMISSION "JUSTICE AND PEACE"

This article deals with three terms or concepts: public life, Catholics, and the freedom of their options. Public life is, as it were, the framework in which the life of everyone, and therefore also that of the Catholic, takes place; and everyone, including the Catholic, always keeps a margin of freedom, by virtue of which he can contribute something personal and original to the public life of the whole of society.

I

The fictitious figure of Robinson Crusoe, alone and non-social on his desert island; and the other figure of Emile from Rousseau's work—half novel, half philosophy—who is born pure and angelic, and remains such until he is corrupted by society; and the theory of Leibniz, according to which every being, and therefore man, also, is for his whole life a nomad enclosed in his incommunicability, are not real facts, but merely extreme interpretations of reality, to which the latter does not seem to give any support. In point of fact, the reality is very different: *man is a social being,* to the extent that even the moments of his conception and birth are social and communitarian. Nor has man only his roots in the community, since his sociality goes much further: his whole being possesses a social dimension, and for this reason, Aristotle *defined* him a "political animal," that is, a being, who lives in a "Polis." If each one of us is not obliged to start out from scratch, this is due to the fact that we begin life rooted in a society, which places us at once at a certain level of culture, the result of the collaboration of generations in the task of dominating the world and life itself. At every moment, in fact, the degree of civilization and prosperity depends on the complexity of the innumerable collaborations that converge on a given point, thus making existence easier.

Any analysis of the most acute presentday problems leads to the same conclusion. When, in these days, we are all up against the increasing rise in prices, to more and more inaccessible peaks, it is not just a question of a mountaineering competition between the prices and the private citizen's wallet, but also of a problem with ramifications all over the world. The relations between capital and work, the elevation of the cultural level, the growth of the world population, recently studied by the Bucharest Conference, the oil and food crisis, the relationships between countries of the first, second and third world . . . these are all public problems, that is to say, problems that concern not just some persons, but communities and peoples, and that must be dealt with, and as far as possible solved, on the community plane.

Let us quote in this connection a paragraph from *Octogesima adveniens:* "The passing to the political dimension also expresses a demand made by the man of today: a greater sharing in responsibility and in decision-making. . . . In *Mater et Magistra* Pope John XXIII stressed how much the admittance to responsibility is a basic demand of man's nature, a concrete exercise of his freedom and a path to his development, and he showed how, in economic life and particularly in enterprise, this sharing in responsibilities should be ensured. Today the field is wider, and extends to the social and political sphere in which a reasonable sharing in responsibility and in decisions must be established and strengthened. Admittedly, it is true that the choices proposed for a decision are more complex; the considerations that must be borne in mind are numerous and foreseeing of the consequences involves risk, even if new sciences strive to enlighten freedom at these important moments" (n. 47).

Let us fix our attention on two fundamental ideas of the text quoted. In the first place, the basic requirement, derived from human nature itself, that all men should take part in decisions that concern them. The other idea concerns the complexity of the problems which are arising and which call for certain conditions to permit responsible participation in decisions connected with them. It is not a question, therefore, of a right (such as the right to preserve one's life) that every man possesses precisely because he is a man, without further requisites. The right to participation, on the contrary, though it is radically a natural one, is given concrete expression by culture: by the overall culture of a society and by personal culture.

On principle, everyone must take part in the study and solution of those problems which he creates, on the one hand, and which concern him, on the other; and that at all community levels. There must consequently be ways open to authentic participation in political life. One of these ways is of fundamental importance, and therefore special mention must be made of it: it is a question of education in general, and more concretely, of education in participation, which must consist mainly in the exercise of this participation.

II

Participation in public life is the consequence of two essentially human dimensions, such as being a member of human society in its various layers and man's capacity to assume gradually his own responsibilities. The *Catholic* knows, first and foremost, that the fact that he is a Catholic does not take away from the fact that he is a man. He can apply to himself the classic sentence: "humani nihil a me alienum puto." Not only can he do so, but also it is his duty.

To neglect the public dimension of existence would be a grave case of inconsistency, since the Catholic's consistency also includes the public dimension of his responsibilities and action. To the extent to which the Catholic, owing to a misconception of Catholicism, were to forget the public dimension of existence and not accept his responsibilities in this field, he would be giving Christianity a Monophysite interpretation.

The ancient Councils—concretely, in this case, Chalcedon and Constantinople II—not merely profess as a dogma of faith that Jesus is true God and true man, "complete God and complete man" on the plane of nature, but also that *on the dynamic plane,* that of the play of active forces, each of the two "forms" or natures acts in accordance with its specific properties, "the form of God operating in accordance with the form of God, and the form of man in accordance with that of man, without confusion or separation." The two inadmissible poles are clearly indicated here: neither Nestorian separation, that is, the dichotomy which consists in dedicating some hours to being a man, after first disconnecting the Christian, and other hours to being a Christian, after first disconnecting the man; nor the Monophysite confusion, that is, the replacement or the devaluation of the human with specifically Christian elements.

The participation of the Catholic in public life must be that which is due to him as a man, and it must not be either less or privileged as compared with the participation of anyone else. On this point, too, the laws of the Incarnation are clear: "being born in the likeness of men, and being found in human form" (Phil. 2, 7).

Within this framework of full humanity, the Catholic, by virtue of his profession, will see certain aspects of human society more clearly. Faith will help him to get his bearings among these problems. Without denying, in fact, the elements of reality present in the community dimension and in its requirements of service for the common good, the dogma of personal survival, on the one hand, and that of the transitoriness of the present world, on the other hand, will help the Catholic to see with greater clarity that stress must be laid on man's personal values. *Gaudium et Spes* puts it as follows: in our days "there is a growing awareness of the exalted dignity proper to the human person, since he stands above all things, and his rights and duties are universal and inviolable. . . The social order and its development must unceasingly work to the benefit of the human person if the disposition of affairs is to be subordinate to the personal realm and not contrariwise, as the Lord indicated when He said that the Sabbath was made for man, and not man for the Sabbath" (n. 26).

In the second place, being a Catholic should lead to a clear emphasis on realism. Last year the Pope recalled this point in the letter sent, in his name, by Cardinal Villot to the LX session of the Social Weeks of

France: "Too often Christians mistrust rigorous analyses and are content with over-emotional reactions, vague impressions, approximations. This does not prevent them from being extremely vulnerable to slogans —that of the *Constantinian era,* for example—and from accepting hastily and uncritically analyses that claim to be scientific. . . The Church does not fear the searching questions raised by authentic human sciences, lucid in their premises, their methods and their results, capable of questioning their hypotheses constantly, comparing them with the evolution of the facts and thus avoiding oversimplifications. Such sciences, at their own level, can be a privileged contribution in order to discern better where human freedom lies (cf. *Octogesima adveniens,* n. 40)."

It is not just a question of the virtue of fortitude or courage. When the Catholic—distinguishing clearly between the objective fact and the subjective explanation or personal interpretation of the facts—endeavors to give more importance to the objective aspect of the fact in itself, he may do so moved by one of the following two reasons of faith: first, because he recognizes that his knowledge, unlike God's, is not the source of reality; and second, because he lets himself be guided by Christian brotherhood, in the sense that, giving priority to the objective aspect in itself, he is practicing one of the forms of love, which consists in endeavoring to put himself in his brother's place, in order to be able to act in all justice.

One last point should be stressed: consideration of the Kingdom of God. The Catholic is one who has been converted to service of the Kingdom of God and who collaborates in its partial implementation in this world. Not that public life can be confused with the Kingdom of God: this is a Monophysite temptation of confusion, which the Catholic must reject, wherever it may come from. But he also knows that seeds of the Kingdom of God are at stake in public life: the promotion of the individual person by means of his complete development, the service of brotherhood among men, action for justice, a greater degree of equality and participation. These are all human values; but the Catholic will attribute an additional value to them, since his faith tells him that, working for these values, he is also working for the Kingdom of God.

In active participation in public life stress will also be laid on the universal dimension of the definitive Kingdom: "Many will come from the east and from the west, and will take their places in the Kingdom of God with Abraham and Isaac and Jacob" (Mt. 8, 11). Modern life has developed this supranational dimension, which must, therefore, be emphasized also in the Catholic's commitment. Hence the importance of the various international Catholic associations, which contribute in so many ways to the formation of awareness of real solidarity and universal responsibilities in the problems of international society.

The way of envisaging this problem depends logically on the attitude assumed with regard to another question, a more general one: what element is most important in man's makeup? A view that emphasizes man's social aspect, tending to consider him as a molecule of a whole, will naturally also stress the limitations of freedom; on the contrary, the view that man is principally a unique and unrepeatable reality, will underline the necessity of giving him space for freedom. As a matter of fact, to approach the problem correctly, it is necessary to start out from an actual fact: in man social and personal elements are united, and this means that in him freedom coexists with some limitations of freedom.

Freedom of option is the adult and mature capacity of self-affirmation, though subject to the influence of social impulses. Collective motivations generally move in the field of items that can be evaluated quantitatively, whereas man's motivations may be of a far higher nature. Freedom and personality will consist precisely in remaining firm in an option of moral and perhaps religious value, even if it is not shared by the society in which one lives and of which one is a member.

The Declaration *Dignitatis humanae* of the Second Vatican Council throws special light on the question of freedom of options. In continuity with the doctrine of the Church, according to which the personal aspect of man must be given precedence over his social dimension, the conciliar document solves the problem of freedom and its limits, by recalling that freedom is an element of the common good and that consequently, not only is it necessary to preserve it, but also to increase it as far as possible. Only if the space of freedom were to clash with other elements of the common good, would its limitation be justified. One of the rights of religious freedom is "that religious bodies should not be prohibited from freely undertaking to show the special value of their doctrine in what concerns the organization of society and the inspiration of the whole of human activity" (cf. n. 4).

CHRISTIAN AUTHENTICITY

At this point, we can draw some conclusions from what has been set forth above. Freedom of option in the field of public life is a value that must be recognized and developed more and more, always safeguarding the rights of others, who are equally entitled to respect of their freedom. If this holds good particularly in the juridical field, its expression on the personal plane will depend mainly on two coordinates: its personal validity will depend on authenticity, which for the Catholic means *Christian authenticity,* within which the principle of the pluralism of options holds good; and its political validity will depend on the realism of the analysis and diagnosis of the situation in question, as well as on the realism of the union of forces, without which a public action is in practice ineffective.

As regards the authenticity of the Christian option, let us recall that Paul VI took it as the key-condition in his recent teaching on the genuine significance of Christian liberation: "Care will have to be taken that the liberation that springs from the Christian faith, as it is professed by the Catholic Church, will keep its logical derivation and its multiple but authentic implementation so that it will succeed in expressing itself in fruitful and original forms, with new vigor and with intelligent appreciation of the needs that the development of civilization, far from satisfying, makes more evident and demanding. Care will have to be taken, we say, that Christian liberation will not be used for mainly political purposes, nor put in the service of ideologies that differ radically from the religious conception of our life, nor controlled by socio-political movements hostile to our faith and our Church, as a worldwide experience shows today, unfortunately. Let us not be blind" (*L'Osservatore Romano,* August 1, 1974).

Once this condition of authenticity is safeguarded and reaffirmed, freedom of option is explicitly recognized: "In concrete situations, and taking account of solidarity in each person's life, one must recognize a legitimate variety of possible options. The same Christian faith can lead to different commitments" (*Octogesima adveniens,* n. 50): where—it should be stressed—authenticity, *Christian* identity, that is "the faith itself," as it is professed objectively by the Catholic Church, is obviously and necessarily safeguarded. This is an obligatory limit of the "legitimacy" of the Catholic's free options, which would not, of course, be legitimate if they conflicted with the requirements and the consistency of faith.

As for political realism, it will be necessary to recall some points of reference. In the first place, the fact that every public problem now becomes a political problem; therefore, to face the public dimension of existence will mean entering the field of political responsibility. This political dimension is growing wider and wider, even reaching the international plane (*Octogesima adveniens,* n. 45).

BEARING WITNESS TO CHRIST

In the second place, collaboration with other men, without conditions or limits, except for those set by one's own identity, as explained above. Vatican II expresses itself as follows: "The common heritage of the gospel and the common duty of Christian witness resulting from it recommend and frequently require the cooperation of Catholics with other Christians. . . . Likewise, common human values not infrequently call for cooperation between Christians pursuing apostolic aims and men who do not profess Christ's name but acknowledge these values. By this dynamic and prudent cooperation, which is of special importance in temporal activities, the laity bear witness to Christ, the Saviour of the world, as well as to the unity of the human family" (Decree *Apostolicam actuositatem,* n. 27).

Catholics' freedom of option in public life is an invitation to conclude these reflections with an appeal to work for the highest result of human freedom: creativity, that is, that point at which man reaches such a development of his faculties that he becomes in a special way an image of God the Creator. And in our times, pregnant with fears, it is more necessary than ever to appeal to this dimension of man's transcendency. It is urgent, therefore, that Catholics should act consciously and positively in public life, in order to find those solutions which promote at the same time respect for human nature, justice in the distribution of property, the complete development of all men and the brotherly solidarity of all peoples.

INTEGRALISM AND CONSISTENCY

by Vincenzo Miano, S.D.B.

SECRETARY OF THE SECRETARIAT FOR NON-BELIEVERS

Today, still, the designation "integralist" (or integrist) and "integralism" (or integrism) is often attributed (less, perhaps, than in other times) to persons or movements, generally in a disparaging sense. Sometimes the term is limited to the theological and doctrinal sphere, but more often it is referred to the attitude assumed by men and movements of Christian inspiration in the social and political field.

It is not easy, moreover, to distinguish clearly the two spheres, since integralism concerns rather the relationship between the Christian view of life, the system of Christian values, and their insertion in public life and, if you like, more generally, the relationship between faith and politics, between the Church and the World.

A definition of integralism would be necessary at this point but it is almost a forlorn hope, since it is not so much a question of a given system of doctrines as of a concern to save the completeness of the doctrine and be consistent with it in life and action. For this reason some people limit themselves to describing the integralist in the persuasion that it is a question rather of a temperamental attitude, an "affective reaction of a neurotic nature." A description of this kind, however, generally given by someone of opposite views, is likely to be one-sided and subjective. This is true also because integralism, as is commonly recognized, is not just one species.

1. Various Definitions

Let us mention here, as an example, the "definition" of O. von Nell-Breuning (*Integralismus,* in *Lexicon fur Theol. und Kirche,* 1960, vol. V, p. 717), accepted also by Fr. Congar: "religious totalitarianism, which wishes to draw from faith (alone) the answer to all the problems of public and private life. Consequently it denies the various cultural environments of the different disciplines, not only absolute but also relative autonomy, and wishes on principle to submit them (or at least subject the activity in which believers express themselves in these spheres) to the *potestas directa* of the Church."

The definition of *Catholic integralism* which we find in the *Dizionario enciclopedico italiano* coincides with the preceding one: "a conception according to which all aspects of political and social life should be postulated and concretely expressed on the basis of the principles of Christian doctrine." The definition adds—and it seems to us interesting—: "more usually in polemics and political writings after the second world war, by integralists are meant those Catholic politicians who, not admitting, or limiting to the minimum, any form of alliance or compromise with other ideologies and movements, struggle for the supremacy of the Christian political ideal and the groups inspired by it."

Rigobello gives a wider definition (since Catholic integralism is not the only kind) in *Enciclopedia filosofica di Gallarate* (2 edit.): "an ethico-political attitude characterized by the desire to implement in a complete form a conception of the world or a program connected with it."

As can be seen, these definitions refer to the relationship between a given conception, "a framework of precise values, worked out completely" (Rigobello) and its implementation. The more strictly doctrinal aspect is not taken into consideration. It seems to us, on the contrary, that in his famous pastoral letter of 1947 *Essor ou declin de l'Eglise,* Cardinal Suhard rightly distinguished between *doctrinal* integralism—which, since it is referred to the values of the past, confuses the integrity of the doctrine with the maintenance of a passing form it has assumed—and *tactical* and *moral* integralism. (The two latter forms have the same root, but one aims at combatting the world, understood as the kingdom of error and sin, waging war on it with the world's own arms, while the other aims at withdrawing from the world, not giving it any thought, insisting rather on personal improvement).

2. Difficulties Met

The difficulty of defining integralism is met with also in the attempt to find synonyms and opposites. Originally *integralism* was opposed to *modernism:* during that period people spoke of *integral* Catholics in the sense of Catholics who fully accepted Catholic dogma, according to the teaching of the councils and popes. But soon the meaning changed: the *integralist* reaction was in opposition to the *minimism* of the modernists and tended to enlarge the claims of dogma, morality and discipline. Today, still on the doctrinal plane, the pair of opposites—integralism-modernism—is often expressed as *traditionalism* (but, in spite of some affinities, the traditionalistic mentality seems to us to have another matrix) or *conservatism* (applied especially to dogmatic formulas) and *progressivism* (dogmatic). In the moral field we also find the binomial *rigorism-laxism,* which, however, does not seem to me to correspond exactly to the opposite tendencies prevailing today. Intransigent, still remaining on the doctrinal plane, is not equivalent to integralist, it seems to us, because intransigence with regard to the known truth, does not in itself exclude recognition of some partial truth possessed by the other.

If we pass now to the practical plane, corresponding to the above-mentioned definitions, integralism is compared with *maximalism, perfectionism, monolithicism,* and is contracted, in turn, with *liberal,* or as is preferred today *democratic* Catholicism; with *tolerance, opening, dialogue;* also from this point of view the opposition between *conservatism* (integralism) and *progressivism* is repeated. The identification between integralism and the rightwing political position (authoritarianism) does not seem to us acceptable, since there is also a leftwing integralism, such as prevails, for example, in countries under a Communist regime.

3. Christian Consistency

As for the interpretation of the phenomenon of integralism and its causes, we find a whole range of explanations. Some people attribute integralism to the need to cling to definitive solutions, and so to fear of the new. Others depict the integralist as one who wishes to decide everything from above and rejects sources coming from below. Others again consider integralism as a false idealism which in its view of the Church separates the human reality from the divine presence. Others, finally, link it with confidence of the illuministic type in the transformation of the world.

In the pastoral letter quoted, Cardinal Suhard contrasted "modernism which sacrifices eternal values, with integralism which maintains obsolete values." With regard to the discipline and action of the Church he pointed out: "To safeguard forms, integralism sacrifices life." In a similar sense Fr. Liege contrasts the integralist spirit and the missionary spirit.

We are convinced that there is some truth in these various characterizations, but it seems to us more fruitful to compare integralism, such as it has been outlined now, and *consistency,* concern with which, as we mentioned at the beginning, plays, in our opinion, an important role in the formation of the integralist mentality. In these observations of ours, it also seems opportune to distinguish between the strictly doctrinal and the strictly practical aspect.

No one denies that consistency is a requisite of thought, not excluding theological thought. Also in the set of revealed truths there is an admirable internal consistency: God who is their Author cannot be in contradiction with himself. That is why, for example, the Dogmatic Constitution on Divine Revelation (n. 12), while stressing the necessity of investigation of the meaning intended by the sacred writers according to historical circumstances and literary forms, affirms that "no less serious attention must be given to the content and unity of the whole of Scripture." When in the Decree on Ecumenism (n. 11) it is said that there exists an order or hierarchy of truths in Catholic teaching, this certainly does not mean that Catholic theologians can neglect or underestimate the less fundamental truths, but only that "they vary in their relationship to the foundation of the Christian faith." This statement implies that every truth must be consistent with the foundation of the faith.

In the doctrinal report he presented on April 30, 1957 to the plenary Assembly of the French Episcopate, Cardinal Lefebvre rightly distinguished, therefore, between integralism and integrity of the faith: "Everyone must take care to preserve the integrity of the faith. But integralism must be firmly rejected: incapable of distinguishing, with the help of the various theological notes, those elements of doctrine that are definitively fixed, and those that are open to improvement or left to the free discussion of theologians, it reaches the point of wishing to stop all progress and seems to take delight in summary condemnations . . . and sweeping statements."

It is not possible, however, to accuse of integralism anyone, who, on the basis of solid reasons, denounces and refutes a theological doctrine as being contrary to dogma; but only one who, refusing to admit legitimate theological pluralism, would like to impose his personal interpretations or opinions on everyone, usurping the task of the Teachers of the Faith.

Doctrinal integralism is manifested more, perhaps, in the difficulty of admitting new formulations and interpretations of the truths of faith, even when they remain faithful to "id quod traditum est." In the Encyclical *Ad Beatissimi* (Nov. 1, 1914) Benedict XV already distinguished in this connection: "Non nova, sed noviter!" Similarly Pius XII said in an address on February 10, 1952 that it was not the moment to seek new principles or assign new purposes and aims—which were already known and certain in their substance—but rather to carry them out as the Church has always tried to do, adapting them to the immediate concrete circumstances. This was the main purpose assigned by John XXIII to the Council (Opening speech on October 11, 1962) in the well-known words: "From the renewed, serene, and tranquil adherence to all the teaching of the Church in its entirety and preciseness, as it still shines forth in the Acts of the Council of Trent and First Vatican Council, the Christian, Catholic and apostolic spirit of the whole world expects a step forward toward a doctrinal penetration and a formation of conscience in faithful and perfect conformity with the authentic doctrine, which, however, should be studied and expounded through the methods of research and through the literary forms of modern thought. The substance of the ancient doctrine of the deposit of faith is one thing, and the way in which it is presented is another preserving at the same time the same sense and the same import."

4. Meaning of Dialogue

No different is the meaning of the dialogue of the Christian faith with modern thought which the reigning Pontiff Paul VI indicated and promoted right from the beginning of his Magisterium—with *Ecclesiam Suam*—not only as "a pastoral policy handed down to us by our predecessors from the last century, starting with the great and wise Leo XIII," but also as the form in which the relationship between the Church and the world is best expressed today; by means of which, that is, the Christian message is inserted "in the circulation of thought, words, culture, morals, trend of humanity, as it lives and bustles about on the face of the earth today."

But the dialogue "must not take the form of an attenuation or diminution of truth," nor can it come to terms with an ambiguous compromise as regards the principles of thought and action that must qualify our Christian profession."

It can be seen, therefore, that the legitimate concern for the consistency and integrity of doctrine cannot be compared in any way with doctrinal integralism.

We now wish to show more clearly the difference between integralism and consistency in the Christian's action.

The Second Vatican Council (*Gaudium et Spes,* n. 34) recognizes not only that the activity with which men seek to improve their conditions of life accords with God's will, but also (n. 36) with the autonomy of earthly affairs in the sense that "created things and societies themselves enjoy their own laws and values which must be gradually deciphered, put to use, and regulated by men." This autonomy is, however, only relative, not absolute, since all created things depend on God and therefore cannot be used without reference to the Creator, all the more so in that human activity is often corrupted by sin (n. 37).

As *Octogesima Adveniens* (n. 50) points out, "in concrete situations . . . a legitimate variety of possible options must be recognized. The same Christian faith can lead to various commitments." Thus the sphere of a legitimate pluralism is recognized, without detriment to due theoretical and practical adherence to the principles and norms which draw their indispensable value from the faith.

Integralism consists both in refusing to recognize the rightful autonomy of earthly affairs in their own specific field, and in rejecting legitimate pluralism where no requirement of Christian faith and morality imposes uniformity in the action of Christians. *Vice versa* it is not integralism but Christian consistency to reject given options which are in contradiction with Christian faith and morality. In the latter case there is no place for a pluralism of options for Christians who wish to remain faithful to the requirements of their faith.

Octogesima Adveniens, therefore, in continuity with the whole teaching of the Church, helps us to distinguish a "politics" in which Christian faith and morality, and therefore the Magisterium of the Church, are not specifically competent, being able to give only indications of principle, in such a way as to leave freedom of various applications and options, from another "politics" in which, on the contrary, the Christian patrimony of faith and morality is at stake, and which calls, therefore—as rightful consistency, not integralism—for a univocal interpretation and application on the part of Christians.[1]

POSITIVE VALUES

It is clear that one cannot just denounce the negative aspects of the "modern world"; it is also necessary to recognize its positive values, to which Christians must open in order to foster their promotion. But it is also clear that neither Pope John nor Vatican II ever denied (they could not have done so) the necessary consistency of the Christian's thought and life, a consistency which cannot, therefore, be accused of integralism.

Thus, for example, John XXIII in his Christmas broadcast in 1959 says that "the pacification that the Church desires, cannot be confused in any way with an abandonment or relaxation of its firmness with regard to ideologies and systems of life that are in proclaimed opposition to Catholic doctrines . . ."

With regard to collaboration with "others who do not have the same view of life," in the Encyclical *Mater et Magistra* he recommends vigilance in order not to be inconsistent with one's moral and religious convictions, while speaking of the readiness "to collaborate sincerely in the implementation of projects that are good by their nature or at least reducible to good."

On the occasion of the controversies on the Referendum for the repeal of the divorce law in Italy, "dissenting" Catholics and others appealed to the teaching of Vatican II, especially as regards the autonomy of earthly affairs, and therefore also of the socio-political order (cf. *Apostolicam Actuositatem,* n. 7, and *Gaudium et Spes, loc. cit.*) and as regards religious freedom, in the document *Dignitatis humanae,* claiming to draw an argument from it to describe the Catholics voting "yes" as anti-democratic and integralist. But wrongly so, on the basis of the teaching of the Council itself.

5. Social Plague

It is hardly necessary to recall that *Gaudium et Spes* n. 47 describes divorce as a social plague, which, together with free-love, polygamy and other disfigurements obscure the dignity of the institution of marriage, often profaned by "excessive self-love, the worship of pleasure, and illicit practices against human generation." "The intimate partnership of married life and love has been established by the Creator and qualified by His laws," the document goes on in n. 48. "It is rooted in the conjugal covenant of irrevocable personal consent." That this is the Catholic doctrine there is no doubt; but the Council teaches furthermore (*ibid,* n. 41) that, on this as on other points, the Gospel, while urging us to acknowledge and esteem the dynamic movements of today by which the rights of man are everywhere fostered, also bids us protect these movements "against any kind of false autonomy. For we are tempted to think that our personal rights are fully ensured only when we are exempt from every requirement of divine law. But this way leads not to the maintenance of the dignity of the human person, but to its annihilation." In other words, the Catholic who is consistent is persuaded to protect human authenticity better.

Ideas about this authenticity differ considerably, it is pointed out however, in the world today. Various humanisms contend the field. Is the Catholic to renounce, in the name of freedom, tolerance and democracy, fighting—with democratic means—for the victory of his own view of life, in particular of society and the family?

The answer to this question comes in several parts. Certainly—and this is the meaning of the conciliar declaration—the dignity of the human person demands free access to the truth: it is not licit, therefore, for anyone to impose a faith or a given ideology on others, just as it is not licit for anyone to harm human rights or to go against the common good. But—referring once more to the example given—who can prove that the indissolubility of marriage harms a fundamental human right, or that it is against the common good? And to support a marriage law that includes indissolubility, is that imposing one's own faith on others?

If Catholics ought to refrain carefully "from any manner of action which might seem to carry a hint of coercion or of a kind of persuasion that would be dishonorable or unworthy," "it comes within the meaning of religious freedom that religious bodies should not be prohibited from freely undertaking to show the special value of their doctrine in what concerns the organization of society and the inspiration of the whole of human activity" (Declaration on Religious Freedom, n. 4). To try to reach these aims—honestly and in a democratic way—is certainly not integralism but only Christian consistency.

It may be objected further that, if Catholics have the right to support certain laws and civil institutions in a democratic way, uniformism is not only not required, but must be excluded. And so some people wish to deduce the legitimacy of dissent in the above-mentioned case or in other similar ones. *Gaudium et Spes* (N. 43) teaches, in fact: "Often enough the Christian view of things will itself suggest some specific solution in certain circumstances. Yet it happens rather frequently, and legitimately so, that with equal sincerity some of the faithful will disagree with others on a given matter."

As has been seen, it certainly cannot be doubted that vast fields where option is permitted are open to Christians. But there are also certainly sectors, and the example given is only one of them, in which Christians, out of consistency with their faith, must be unanimous, since they must "strive to discharge their earthly duties conscientiously and in response to the gospel spirit." "They are mistaken who . . . shirk their earthly responsibilities . . . Nor are they any less wide of the mark who imagine they can plunge themselves into earthly affairs in such a way as to imply that these are altogether divorced from the religious life. This split between the faith which many profess and their daily lives deserves to be counted among the more serious errors of our age" (*ibid.*). It is always an appeal to Christian consistency that is made, and this consistency is all the more urgent when the Pastors of the Church expressly ask for it: the Council, in fact, (*ibid.*) asks us to give "close attention to the teaching authority of the Church." In this case, there is an obvious failure to apply what the pastoral Constitution stresses firmly (against integralism), that is, that "no one is allowed in the aforementioned situations to appropriate the Church's authority for his opinion." "No" to integralism, therefore, but "yes" to consistency!

It was not our intention to enter into controversy with anyone. We have merely tried to distinguish between two deeply different attitudes. According to the teaching of the Council, Christians must be open to cooperate with all the legitimate, and often exalting, conquests of the modern world. But, faithful to the spirit of the Gospel, they cannot accept all the acclaimed "civil conquests" as objectively such.

---

[1] See nos. 4-5; 7 (at the end; permanent, eternal truths); 18 (against contraception and abortion; adoption of adequate measures, provided they are in conformity with the demands of moral law); 24 (various models of organization of political society); 26 (the Christian who wishes to live his faith in political action . . . cannot, without contradicting himself, give his adherence to ideological systems that are opposed radically or on substantial points to his faith and his conception of man); 27 (the Christian faith takes up a position above and sometimes contrary to ideologies); 30 (conformity to the dictates of reason); 31 (ideologies incompatible with the faith); 36 (the Christian will draw principles and criteria from the sources of his faith and from the teaching of the Church . . . Beyond every system . . . he will affirm, at the very center of his options, the originality of the Christian contribution to the advantage of a positive transformation of society); 46 (while recognizing the autonomy of the political reality, Christians will endeavor to reach a consistency between their options and the Gospel and to bear, though in the midst of a legitimate pluralism, a personal and collective testimony to the seriousness of their faith . . .); 48 (quoting *Populorum Progressio:* If the task of the Hierarchy is to teach and interpret authentically the moral principles to be adopted in this field/of the temporal order/, it is for laymen . . . to instill the Christian spirit into the mentality and morals, the laws and structures of their community of life); 49 (involved in various movements in which, alongside legitimate aspirations, there are more ambiguous trends, the Christian must make a discerning choice and avoid committing himself to collaborations that are not controlled and are contrary to the principles of true humanism . . . If in fact he wishes to have a specific function as a Christian in conformity with his faith—a function that non-believers themselves expect of him—he must be careful, in his active commitment, to elucidate his own motivations, etc.); 51 (Christian organizations must express the concrete requirements of Christian faith . . .).

PROJECTION OR NULLIFICATION OF THE EVANGELICAL PRINCIPLES IN HISTORY

by Franz Mussner

PROFESSOR OF BIBLICAL THEOLOGY AT THE UNIVERSITY OF REGENSBURG

Principles are "guiding-ideas" that have the purpose of giving order to the thought and action of man and humanity. For this reason principles are also "regulating ideas," "axioms" or "maxims." The "evangelical principles" are principles that have been brought into the world by the Gospel. The "evangelical principles" have, in the world and its history, the function of "yeast" which must leaven the whole dough (cf. Mt. 13, 33). This is the "founder's" will. Three "guiding-ideas" in particular are stressed in the Gospel: Brotherhood, Love, Freedom. By the "Gospel" is meant here not only the four canonical gospels, but the whole of the New Testament.

1. First Principle: Brotherhood

Jesus says to his disciples: "You are all brothers" (Mt. 23, 5). It is particularly the evangelist Matthew who consistently sees in the community of Jesus a "community of brothers." "Church" is for him a community of brothers, in relationship, of course, with Jesus and his Father. Jesus himself is included in this community of brothers (cf. Mt. 12, 50 and 28, 10) and this community is understood in a universal sense (25, 40, 45). The brotherhood of the disciplies is extended to the brotherhood of all men. In the passage that deals with "the true kinsmen of Jesus" (Mt. 12, 46-50), by "brothers" are understood not blood relations, but those who do God's will. With this Jesus breaks "clan particularism" and understands "brotherhood" in a universal sense. The consequences that result for the community are shown in Mt. 18, 15-35. The passage deals with the fundamental organization of the "Kingdom of God," with the behavior of brothers to one another. The fundamental demand is reconciliation and constant availability for comprehension: in this way peace is preserved in the community. Also the concepts of "servant," "serve," are associated with the concept of "brotherhood." "Brothers" must "serve one another" (cf. 23, 11).

To speak of one's "brother" is also to speak of one's "neighbor." In the Synoptic tradition a universalizing tendency is seen in this connection, too, especially in the parable of the good Samaritan (Lk. 10, 29-37). What the parable offers as Jesus' teaching on one's "neighbor" is as follows: man's "neighbor" is not his compatriot or even his co-religionist—the Jews in Jesus' time did not consider the Samaritans compatriots or co-religionists. Your "neighbor" is rather anyone you meet in life. For Jesus it is not ties of blood, origin, race, culture, "party," "denomination," which make the other my neighbor, but rather loving and helpful dedication to the other. The conception of "neighbor" in Jesus' teaching is something that crosses the whole of mankind with all its barriers and its natural and artificial particularisms and continually overcomes them. In this way Jesus combats the permanent tendency to define and delimit *a priori* the circle of those who are our "neighbors." The ideologists of this world are continually proclaiming doctrines about "our neighbors" which are in clear contrast with the doctrine of Jesus. He who regulates his feeling and his action in accordance with the teaching of Jesus, builds up justice in the world.

According to the apostle Paul, Christ is "the eldest of many brothers" (Rom. 8, 29; cf. also Heb. 2, 11). Christ is the "eldest" not only as the risen Christ, but also as the crucified Christ. As such he is in solidarity with all those who are crucified, that is, with all the suffering, with all those who groan, who are despised, but who at the same time hope, whose hope will be carried out in the resurrection of the dead. In this way the concept of brotherhood remains completely fixed to Christ, whose spirit is in us and invokes the "Father!" in us. The great brotherhood of men is not, however, something which is to come, a pure utopia of the future. There already exists one who unites men in brotherhood, the "second" or "last Adam" (1 Cor. 15, 45, 47). As (second or last) Adam, Christ is the brother of all. "In this way there springs from Christ, together with a new way of being man, also a new human brotherhood, which exceeds and replaces the old one" (J. Ratzinger). All men will become brothers in Christ; they must already be brothers in the Christian community, if the latter wishes to be a sign in the world.

It is in this context that Paul can announce that for those who, through baptism are "in Christ," the old distinctions—which, nevertheless, strongly characterize this period of history—such as "Jews," "Greeks," "slaves," "freemen," have no longer any value, but only "a new creation" (cf. Gal. 6, 15; 1 Cor. 12, 13; Col. 3, 11). Here, too, the eschatological future shows itself as a real sign in the world. The differences that were so important before, that divided men into many different groups and beings according to nationality, social and sexual factors, are already outdated and will disappear definitively in the new creation. Then all men will be brothers. The concept of the brotherhood of all is one of those principles that were brought into the world by the Gospel.

2. Second Principle: Love

The principle of *love* is indissolubly connected with that of brotherhood. Where there is brotherhood there must be mutual love, and love on its side nourishes brotherhood. In the understanding of the New Testament love is not enlightened philanthropy, but imitation of God's love for men: "Let us love one another since love comes from God"; "we are to love, then, because he loved us first" (1 John 4, 7, 19). Love of God and love of one's neighbor are the essence of the whole law (Mk. 12, 28-31). The commandment to love one's neighbor (Lev. 19, 18) is compared by Jesus to the commandment to love God (Mt. 22, 39). God's love for men is universal love which embraces the good and the bad, the just and the unjust (Mt. 5, 45); consequently also our love for our neighbor cannot exclude anyone, but must embrace everyone. He who loves his friends only, is no different from "sinners" (Lk. 6, 32 f.). Jesus puts reconciliation above religious duties (Mt. 5, 23 f), love of one's neighbor above worship (9, 13; 12, 7) and the commandment of the sabbath (Mk. 3, 1-6; Lk. 13, 10-17). Love is the sign by which the true Christian is recognized (Jn. 13, 35). All the commandments are summed up in the commandment to love one's neighbor Rom. 13, 8; Gal. 5, 13). Love is therefore superior to all charisms (1 Cor. 13, 1); what is more, charisms are of no use if they are not accompanied by love (13, 2 f). In the letter of St. James, the command to love one's neighbor is the "supreme law" (2, 8); so that even faith without works of love is dead (2, 26) and does not possess any force of justification. In this James is in full agreement with Paul, according to whom faith must be active through love (Gal 5, 6). For the New Testament love is *the* evangelical principle par excellence.

3. Third Principle: Freedom

The third evangelical principle that we wish to name here is the principle of *freedom*. The Gospel is a call to freedom. This was clearly shown by the apostle Paul particularly. "When Christ freed us, he meant us to remain free" (Gal. 5, 1). This clear sentence of the Apostle takes on the role of a program for man: the salvific work of liberation has as its aim the freedom of man and of the whole creation (cf. Rom. 8, 21). Liberation and freedom are the ultimate purpose of the whole of salvation. For the Apostle, Christ is the great liberator.

From what did Christ liberate us? The answer that emerges from Pauline theology as a whole is the following: Christ frees us from the *law* as the way to salvation. The law (and for Paul, law does not comprise only the ritual practices of the Torah) which, for the Old Testament, is power of Life, becomes for Paul practically power of death (Rom. 7, 10; Gal. 3, 12); it becomes "the power of sin" (1 Cor. 15, 56). Man living "in the flesh" was too weak to carry out the severe commands of the law, so that, through the law, he did not reach the space of freedom, but fell into the trap of the power of sin and death. By "law" Paul understands in the first place, of course, the Torah and its rabbinical explanations. But as the letter to the Galatians shows, it applies also to "slavery to the elemental principles" of the pagans (Gal. 4, 3, 9). If the Jew expects salvation from service of the Law, the pagan expects it from "service of the elements." For Paul, on the contrary, the eschatological salvation of man and the world comes only from faith in the crucified and risen Christ, the grace of God become man:

"God's justice that was made known through the Law has now been revealed outside the Law . . . through faith to everyone" (Rom. 3, 21 f).

Does this doctrine of the Apostle aim at a world completely free from every power? No. Because the believer receives "another" Lord, "him who rose from the dead to make us productive for God" (Rom. 7, 4). This "new" Lord of the world brings to the world with his work of liberation the principles of brotherhood and love, because his dominion is the rule of love. We are still "slaves," it is true, but "slaves" serving in the new being of the Spirit, not in the old one of the letter (Rom. 7, 6). In this way the relationships of power are completely changed (cf. also Rom. 6, 22).

Christ also frees from the deadly power of *sin*. Sin is for the Apostle a sovereign power (cf., for example, Rom. 7, 11). Furthermore there is, for the Apostle, an indissoluble link between sin and law. Because it was just through the law that sin became manifest and recognizable in its essence (Rom. 7, 7, 13). Sin is what, in the last analysis, evil carries out in man (Rom. 7, 18-20). Sin makes man a "prisoner" against his best intentions and in spite of his goodwill (Rom. 7, 23). To express it in modern terms, owing to the power of sin man falls "into alienation." Only through liberation from sin can man become himself again. His dignity as a person is fully restored at the same time. For freedom is part of being a person in the full sense.

Christ also frees us from *death* as the eschatological power of evil. "When the commandment came, sin revived and I died" (Rom. 7, 9 f). The law, sin and death are, therefore, indissolubly connected. The death of which he speaks is "real" death, definitive separation from communion with God. But this death shows its terrible essence also in physical death. Paul, of course, is well aware that our body is still subject to physical death, but he also knows the new being in Christ who survives earthly death and who is thus in contrast with eternal death.

According to Rom. 8, 21, creation will one day be "freed from its bondage to decay, to enjoy the glorious freedom of the children of God." The future liberation of the whole of creation which is preannounced by the Apostle here, has a double purpose: a negative one: "liberation" from the general submission to death, and a positive one: "liberation" for that freedom which in the Lord's Parousia will appear as "the glory of the children of God" after their resurrection from the dead. "With this there comes hope, not only for the believer, but for the whole of creation. For, since Adam's fall, the world lacks nothing but eschatological freedom, which alone can signify salvation for it too" (E. Kasemann). The world aims at freedom, which must not, of course, be confused with autonomy. Paul does not individualize salvation, as Gnosticism once did and as existentialism does again.

The freedom for which Christ freed us is against individualism also because, as Paul teaches, it is liberation through love: "do not let this freedom give a foothold to the flesh. Serve one another, rather, in works of love" (Gal. 5, 13). The concepts "the flesh" and "love" characterize two opposed worlds. While love is expressed in service of man, the flesh is expressed as a selfish withdrawal and narcissistic pursuit. Only he who loves is really free, because he is free of himself.

What Paul presents as a theological theory, had already been shown previously in the "practice" of Jesus. His acceptance of sinners, his meals with them, his miracles, are visible signs of the Kingdom of God, which is already making its appearance with him. In these signs the salvation that appears with the Kingdom of God is manifested. But this salvation is essentially liberation: liberation from the chains of sin, liberation from the shackles of obsession, disease and death. Also the clear criticism of concrete legalistic life prepared the way for the theology of Paul's law; it, too, aims at freedom. Jesus' radical reduction of the laws of the Torah to a few principles which are connected with the commandment to love God and one's neighbor, leaves a new space for freedom, in which the future appears.

4. Have The Principles Been Effective?

Three great "evangelical principles" connected with one another are clearly seen: Brotherhood (justice), love and freedom. Now the question we wish to ask is: how effective have these principles been in the Church and in the world? Have they been effective in the history of mankind after Jesus and Paul, or not? Many sceptics and critics of our time would deny that they have had a great influence in history. Would it not be true that the three principles of the French revolution, "freedom, equality, brotherhood" have had far more effect on history than the three fundamental principles of the Gospel? But is it really true? Or should it be stated that the principles expressed by the French revolution could never have been expressed in this way without the Gospel and knowledge of its three fundamental principles?

It is true that in the thought of the ancient Greeks there was present a preparation for the Gospel, a "praeparatio evangelica," as the Fathers of the Church themselves realized, even as regards the idea of freedom. But did the Greeks know that freedom and the future, and freedom and the salvation of the world, are closely connected? And if, according to Hegel, "the history of the world . . . is progress in consciousness of freedom," he himself expressly states, on the other hand, that it was only through Christianity that this consciousness of freedom was awakened in the world. With the French revolution the three evangelical principles became political principles, which subsequently had an enormous influence on history, particularly through Marxism. But in this way the evangelical principles of brotherhood (justice), love and freedom have been drained of their meaning. As a matter of fact they have been torn out of their "context," to which the reality of "God" belongs above all, and put in another context, that of the (permanent) revolution of the (secularized) world. What is lost particularly in this new context is love, and without it the world becomes unbearable, history becomes a "butcher's bench."

To what extent is the Church guilty for the way things have turned out? The Church cannot avoid this question and in this case, too, must be ready for the continual conversion demanded by Jesus. Her task is to make ever greater efforts in theory and in practice so that *love* will be continually recognized as the fundamental principle in human reality, without which brotherhood and freedom are in the long run, impossible in the world. The Church must see to it that her voice is listened to in a world in which the love of many seems to be growing cold (cf. Mt. 24, 12). Only love makes the world a human world! The Church can give clear signs and these signs must be determined by imitation of Jesus. These signs must be concrete ones and so it is a good thing, in conclusion, to mention a name which has become an example of what the Church can and must do in the world today: Mother Teresa of Calcutta. Her exemplary work shows that the evangelical principles of brotherhood, love and freedom can produce a great effect even in the world of today and can still leave their mark on history.

MAGISTERIUM OF THE CHURCH, FAITH, MORALITY

by Joseph Ratzinger

PROFESSOR OF DOGMATIC THEOLOGY AT REGENSBURG UNIVERSITY AND MEMBER OF THE THEOLOGICAL COMMISSION

1. Survey of the Problem

The crisis of faith, which is making itself increasingly felt in Christendom, is more and more clearly seen to be also a crisis in awareness of the fundamental values of human life. On the one hand it is nourished by the moral crisis of mankind and on the other hand it has repercussions on the latter, making it more acute. When the attempt is made to survey the panorama of the present discussions on this matter, strange contradictions are met with, which, however, are closely connected with one another. On the one hand, particularly since the meeting of the World Council of Churches at Upsala, there is an increasingly clear tendency to define Christianity primarily as "orthopraxis" and not as "orthodoxy." There are various reasons for this. Reference should perhaps be made to the seriousness of the racial problem for American Christian communities. Their religion has not succeeded in breaking down the barriers of separation and therefore the validity of faith itself seems to be questioned, since it has not been able to bring to life the love that is the root of the Gospel. In this way a practical question becomes the touchstone of the intrinsic value of doctrine, the proof of what is Christian: where "orthopraxis" is so glaringly absent, "orthodoxy" seems questionable.

Another origin of the trend towards "praxis" lies in the various movements of "political theology," which on their side have different motives. Common to them all is great perplexity due to the questions raised by Marxism. The concept of "truth" is regarded here with suspicion or at least as being without value. To this extent this theory is identified with the fundamental feeling that gives rise to positivism. Truth is considered unattainable and its proclamation only an alibi for group interests, which are thus consolidated. Only praxis can decide (still according to this view) the value or lack of value of theories. So if Christianity wishes to make some contribution to the construction of a better world, it should create a better praxis—not seek truth as a theory, but reestablish it as a reality.

The claim that Christianity should become "orthopraxis" of joint activities for a more human future and leave orthodoxy aside as unfruitful or harmful, takes on here a far more fundamental character than in the case of the pragmatic standpoint described above. It is clear at the same time that both positions tend to unite and strengthen each other. In both cases there remains little room for a magisterium, although if these principles were applied consistently it should appear again in a different form. Certainly, a magisterium that wished to formulate a preconstituted truth with regard to correct human praxis and wished to measure praxis by this truth, would fall on the negative side of reality as an obstacle to creative, forward-looking praxis. It would appear as the expression of interests concealed under the label of "orthodoxy" and opposed to the advance of the history of freedom. On the other hand it is admitted that praxis needs reflection and well thought out tactics, for which reason the tie between Marxist practice and the "magisterium" of the party is perfectly logical.

The movement that would like to define and realize Christianity as orthopraxis is opposed at the other end (and in fact often passes into it suddenly) by the position that maintains there is no specific Christian morality; on the contrary Christianity must take its norms of behavior every time from the anthropological knowledge of its own age. Faith does not offer any independent principle of moral norms but on this point refers strictly to reason; anything that is not guaranteed by reason would not be supported by faith. This assertion is justified with the statement that, even in its historical sources, the faith did not develop any morality of its own but followed the practical reason of contemporaries in the different periods. This can be seen already in the Old Testament, where value concepts from the time of the patriarchs to sapiential literature were in continual change, conditioned by contact with the development of the moral concepts of collateral cultures. Nowhere can there be found, they say, a moral sentence limited only to the Old Testament, of which it could be said that it is the result exclusively of faith in Jehovah; in the moral field everything was borrowed elsewhere. According to this theory, this applies also to the New Testament: the virtues and vices listed in the Pauline epistles reflect Stoic morality and in this way are the acceptance of the rational canons of human behavior at that time. For this reason their value lies not in the content, but in their structure: as a reference to reason as the only source of moral norms.

It need hardly be said that also with this point of departure there is no room for an ecclesiastical Magisterium in the moral field. For norms essentially based on the tradition of faith would, according to this thesis, spring from the misunderstanding that the teachings of the Bible are absolute and perennial indications while they are only a reference to the positions reached at different moments by the knowledge attained by reason.

It is clear that, in both cases, it is a question of fundamental problems of Christianity, which cannot be dealt with sufficiently in a few pages. In the first case, when the interpretation of Christianity as "orthopraxis" is made not only on the pragmatic plane but also on the plane of principles, the problem in discussion is truth and above all the fundamental question of what reality is. With the problem of being it is a question, in the last analysis, of the first article of the faith, even though people are not always specifically aware of the fact and positions are seldom pushed to their radical extremes. In the second case it seems to be a question above all of a particular historical problem, the historical origin of certain biblical teaching. A closer examination shows that the problem is a more fundamental one, namely how to determine what is specifically Christian in view of the changing historical forms of Christiianity. At the same time there is at stake the problem of the interpretation of the relationships between faith and reason and between faith and man in general; and finally, in particular, the question of the possibility and limits of reason as compared with faith.

2. First Counter-Deductions

Let us begin with the most obvious and simplest things and then go on to the specific question, that is, the problem of the historical origin of biblical teaching in the moral field. In the first place it is necessary to examine a general methodological question. The hypothesis that what is received can never become one's own, is quite simply false. We know this from our own life. The theological principle "What hast thou that thou hast not received?" (1 Cor. 4, 7) is evident even on the purely human plane; but we know it also from the whole history of culture: the dimension of a culture is shown by its capacity of communication, its capacity to give and take, yes, take, receive and assimilate. The originality of Christianity in the moral field does not lie in the sum of principles which have no parallels elsewhere (if there are any such principles, which is very problematic). It is not possible to distill what is specifically Christian in this field by taking away everything that was borrowed from others. Christian originality consists rather in the new overall conception into which man's quest and aspiration was directed by faith in the God of Abraham, in the God of Jesus Christ. The reference of morality to pure reason is in no way proved by the fact that the moral teaching of the Bible has its origin in other cultures or philosophical thought. Such an assertion would represent a short circuit of thought that can no longer be tolerated. What is decisive is not the fact that these principles can be found elsewhere, but only the problem of the place they do or do not occupy in the spiritual structure of Christianity. It is this point, therefore, that must be studied next.

Here, too, let us begin with a very simple observation. It is incorrect from the historical point of view to say that Christianity took over at all periods the morality of its contemporary environment, that is, the degree of moral knowledge reached by reason. For "the environment" as such and a unitarian "morality" all ready to be taken over, did not exist. We see rather that, amid tensions that were often highly dramatic, the elements of the juridico-moral tradition of the surrounding world were divided into those which, corresponding to the figure of Jahweh, could be assimilated by Israel and those which, on the basis of its representation of God, had to be rejected. The battle of the prophets is in the last analysis connected with this problem. Whether we think of Nathan, who forbids David to take on the form of a despotic Oriental potentate, free to take his neighbor's wife if he likes; or of Elijah, who, defending Naboth's right, defends the right guaranteed by the God of Israel, against the absolutism of kings; or of Amos, who in his battle for fair wages for workers and dependents, is mainly defending the image of the God of Israel—it is the same thing. Even the whole conflict between Jahweh and Baal cannot be reduced to a pure "dogmatic" question but is connected with the inseparable unity of faith and life, which is at stake here: the option for one God or for the gods is in every case a life decision.

3. Three Examples of the Union of Faith and Morality

a) The Ten Commandments

With these arguments we have now reached the heart of the matter, which we will now try to clarify with three characteristic examples. Let us cast a glance first of all at the Ten Commandments (Ex. 20, 1-17; Dt. 5, 6-21), one of the central formulations of Jahweh's will regarding Israel, by which the morality of Israel and of the Church has always been renewed. It can be shown without any doubt that these Commandments have models both in the Egyptian lists of crimes that must not be committed and in the lists of questions of Babylonian exorcism. Even the introductory formula: "I am the Lord thy God," is not completely new. Yet it gives the "ten laws" a new significance: they are connected with faith in the God of Israel, the God of the Covenant and his will. The "Ten Commandments" indicate what is the essence of faith in God, of acceptance of the covenant with Jahweh. At the same time they define the image of God himself, whose essence is manifested in his will. This fact connects the Ten Commandments with the fundamental revelation of God in Exodus 3, since here, too, the manifestation of God is expressed concretely in the manifestation of his will in ethical matters: He has heard the groans of the oppressed and has come to liberate them. With these words the introduction to the Ten Commandments is connected both with the version in Exodus 20 and with its repetition in Deuteronomy: Jahweh presents himself as the God who has brought Israel out of Egypt, the house of bondage. This means that the Ten Commandments are, in Israel, part of the very conception of God. They do not take their place alongside the faith, alongside the alliance; they show who the God is with whom Israel is in alliance.

Connected with this is the particular development of the conception of "holy" in biblical religion. From the standpoint of the history of religion, "holy" indicates in the first place the "being-quite-different" of divinity, its specific atmosphere, from which the particular rules for relations with divinity are drawn. In Israel, too, this was so to begin with as a large number of biblical passages show. But when Jahweh presents his particularity, his "being-quite-different," in the Ten Commandments, it becomes clear (and the prophets make people more and more aware of it) that the "being-quite-different" of Jahweh, his holiness, is a moral greatness to which man's moral action must correspond, according to the Ten Commandments. The conception of holiness, as the specific category of the divine, merges, even in those ancient strata of tradition to which the Ten Commandments belong, with the conception of morality, and this is precisely the novelty, the singularity of this God and his holiness. But here, too, lies the new value that morality acquires, which determines the criterion of choice in the dialogue with the ethics of peoples, until there arises that lofty concept of holiness which, in the Old Testament anticipates the divine figure of Jesus: "I will not execute my fierce anger . . . for I am God and not man, the Holy One in your midst . . ." (Hosea, 11, 9). "There can be no doubt that with the proclamation of the Ten Commandments in Israel, there takes place the election of Israel, says Gerhard v. Rad in his *Theology of the Old Testament*. He also presents the consequences of this correlation on the liturgical life of Israel. All this does not mean, of course, that right from the beginning the Ten Commandments were understood in all their deep significance and that mere enunciation at once brings with it essential moral knowledge. The history of the interpretation of the Ten Commandments from the earliest times to their reformulation in Jesus' Sermon on the Mount, shows rather that they could and were obliged to bring about an even deeper understanding of the divine will and thereby also of God and man himself. What has been said makes it clear that though individual parts of the Ten Commandments come from an environment outside Israel, this does not prove that they do not belong to the faith of the covenant. After all, this assertion could be made only by starting from the premise that the reason of peoples and the revelation of God are paradoxical, unconnected by any analogy, that is, starting out from a precise position about the relationship between revelation and reason, which the biblical texts do not show to be true, but on the contrary clearly show to be false.

b) The name "Christian"

Let us choose a second example, this time in the field of early Christianity, in which it is again a question, as for Israel in the Ten Commandments, of a central issue: the meaning of the words "Christian" and "Christianity" at the time when the Church was coming into being. From Acts 11, 26 we know that this name was given to the community of believers in Antioch for the first time. Although the origin and initial meaning of the denomination are still debatable in the present state of the sources, it is nevertheless clear that it at once took on an ironical meaning and that it became in Roman law the designation of a crime liable to punishment: Christians are members of Christ's conspiring sect. From Hadrian onwards, therefore, to bear the name "Christian" is expressly declared a penal offense. Peterson has shown that the accusations against the Christians, as found in Suetonius and Tacitus, are part of the political propaganda "carried on against real or presumed conspirators." Yet already in the time of Ignatius of Antioch we see the Christians taking over this dangerous word to designate themselves, proud to bear it and to prove themselves worthy of it. What happens when this insulting name, liable to penal penalties, is consciously assumed and borne?

There are two possible answers. In the first place there is in St. Ignatius a marked theology of martyrdom, which leads to assumption of the name which itself involves martyrdom. Communion with Jesus Christ, which for him is faith, means in the eyes of the world participation in a conspiracy for which the punishment is death. This is for the bishop of Antioch an outside view, which gets a glimpse of what there is inside, but in a form completely different from the reality: communion with Jesus is, in fact, participation in his death and only in this way also in his life (*Magnesians,* 5, 1 f.) This means: the conception of the common conspiracy of Christians with Christ contains this element of truth, that Christians do not take over just a theory from Jesus, but participate in his choice of life and death and repeat it in their own way. "Since we have become his disciples, we must learn to live in a Christian way" (*Magn*. 10, 1). In this sense, for the Syrian martyr bishop Christianity is completely "orthopraxis," it means imitating Jesus' way of life. But what is this way of life? This question leads to a second consideration. For the pagan the word "Christian" means a conspirator, who is represented according to the patterns of political propaganda as guilty of terrible crimes ("flagitia"), in particular, "hatred of mankind" and dissoluteness "stuprum"). Against this view Ignatius uses a play on words which was used for a long time in Christian apolegetics. In Greek phonetics the word "chrestos" (good) was (and is) pronounced with the "i": christos. Ignatius takes advantage of this when he precedes the sentence "let us learn to live in accordance with Christianity" with the words "let us not be insensitive to its goodness (chrestotes, pronounced christotes)" (*Magn*. 10, 1). The conspiracy of the Christian is a conspiracy to be "chrestos," a conspiracy to do good. One hundred years later Tertullian still says: "The word Christian is taken from the expression to be good" (*Apol*. III, 5; *Ad Nat*. I, 3). The connection between conception of God and moral idea, which we found in the Ten Commandments, is repeated here in Christianity in a highly sublime and demanding way. The name "Christian" means communion with Christ, but for that very reason, the willingness to accept the martyrdom of good. Christianity is a conspiracy to do good. The theological and moral qualities are inseparably bound up with the name and, even deeper, with the essential concepts of Christianity.

c) Apostolic teaching

But with this Ignatius and the early Christian theology that follows him are strictly on the plane of apostolic preaching, which we will now take as our third example. The close connection between faith and "imitation" of the Apostle, which is "imitation" of Jesus Christ, is characteristic of St. Paul's preaching. The first Epistle to the Thessalonians is particularly precise in this respect: ". . . we gave you a pattern of how you ought to live . . . live by that pattern. You have not forgotten the instructions we gave you by the command of the Lord Jesus" (1 Thess. 4; 1 ff.). The "live" belongs to tradition, the order does not come from just anywhere, but from the Lord Jesus; the specifications that follow are taken from the Ten Commandments and explain them in a Christian way, adapted to the special situation of the Thessalonians.

At this point it might be objected that here the main question concerns only the formal intention of "good," which is beyond all doubt characteristic of Christianity. But the essential problem: "in what does this good consist?" is not answered by theological sources, but decided on each occasion by reason and time. And then reference can be made to a text that seems to confirm this, such as Phil 4, 8: "Finally, brothers, fill your minds with everything that is true, everything that is noble, everything that is good and pure, everything that we love and honor, and everything that can be thought virtuous or worthy of praise." These, it is said, are concepts of popular philosophy, in which accepted standards of good are clearly proposed to Christians as their standards. But it could at once be answered that the text goes on to say: "Keep doing all the things that you learnt from me and have been taught by me and have heard or seen that I do" (4, 9). It could be added that after all this passage is a commentary on 2, 5: "In your minds you must be the same as Christ Jesus" where we find the same necessary connection between Jesus' way of thinking and Christian existence as we came across it in Ignatius.

But on the historical and objective plane it is necessary to go deeper. It is certainly true that Paul, here as elsewhere, refers to that moral knowledge that awakened the conscience of the pagans, and it is true that he identifies this knowledge with God's true law, according to the principles set forth in Rom. 2, 15. But that does not mean that the *Kerygma* is reduced here to a generic exhortation to adhere to what is considered good by reason in each individual case. Two facts contradict this view: 1) historically speaking, this "reason of time" has never existed and never will. What Paul found was not a precise position of research on good, which he could just take over, but a confusion of contradictory positions of which Epicurus and Seneca are only two examples. This being so, it was not possible to proceed by accepting these positions. It was necessary, on the contrary, to make a decisive and critical separation, in which the Christian faith formed its new options in accordance with the Old Testament standards and with the "way of thinking of Jesus Christ." These options were condemned by the outside world as "conspiracy," but were only all the more resolutely considered as the real "good" by Christians themselves.

Contrary to the above-mentioned opinion is, secondly, the fact that for Paul conscience and reason are not two changeable standards, which say one thing today and another tomorrow. Conscience proves it is what it is precisely by saying the same things as God said in the covenant with the Jews; as conscience, it reveals what is abiding and thus leads necessarily to the way of thinking of Jesus Christ. The real thought of the apostle Paul is seen most clearly, perhaps, in the first chapter of the Epistle to the Romans, where that connection of morality with the conception of God, which we found to be a characteristic of the Old Testament, is repeated. Lack of the notion of God brings about the moral deficiency of the pagan world; conversion to God in Jesus Christ coincides with conversion to imitation of Jesus Christ. Paul had already developed the same thought in I Thessalonians: the non-holiness of pagans is due to the fact that they do not know God; God's will is "sanctification," which is received, in the moral sense, directly in the message of grace. Anyone who reads Paul's epistles carefully will easily see that apostolic preaching is not a moralizing appendage the contents of which could be changed, but is the concrete designation of what faith is and is therefore linked indissolubly with its central point. In this the Apostle is only following the example of Jesus who, in the introduction and conclusion of his teaching on the kingdom of God had connected indissolubly this central subject of his preaching with the fundamental moral decisions that come from the image of God and are closely linked with him.

4. Faith—Morality—Magisterium

The reference to apostolic teaching with the connection between faith and morality brings up the matter of the Magisterium. For the apostolic epistles are an exercise of the teaching authority. In them Paul takes up a position "magisterially" also on the moral aspect of faith. The same applies to all the epistles in the New Testament and to the Gospels, which are full of moral instructions, and also to the Apocalypse. In his teaching, Paul does not theorize about human rationality, but sets forth the inner necessity of grace, as H. Schlier has pointed out forcibly in his fine article on the originality of Christian teaching (*Besinnung auf das Neue Testament,* 1964, pp. 340-357). Actually, although the apostle is convinced he has the authority (2 Cor. 8, 8), he does not use the form of explicit command too often (1 Thess. 4, 10 f.; other texts in Schlier, p. 342). He does not want to correct the Christian communities with reproofs and the rod, as teachers corrected children in ancient times—he prefers fatherly persuasion in the Christian family. But precisely by doing so he makes it clearly understood that behind his words is the mercy of God himself calling. In his exhortation it is grace that exhorts, it is God that exhorts; it is not a variable accessory to the Gospel, but is guaranteed by the authority of the Lord, even when it is not presented in the form of a command or doctrinal decision. The same can be said when the central themes of his doctrine are considered: salvation in Christ, baptism, the communion of the Body of Christ, the last judgment. The line of demarcation drawn by grace in regard to the life of those who do not know God is quite clear: it is abstention from wantonness, greed, envy and quarrelsomeness; inclination to obedience, patience, truth, trust and joy: in these attitudes the fundamental command of love is unfolded.

What we see in Paul is continued in the writings of the successors of the apostles, in which the apostolic doctrine is explained in a way suited to the situation (Schlier, 343). This means that, for the New Testament, the ecclesiastical Magisterium does not end with the time of the Apostles. The Church therefore remains apostolic also in the post-apostolic era, and it is her permanent task to see to it that the legitimate successors of the apostles defend the unchangeability of the apostolic doctrine. Luke sets this forth expressly in the crisis of transition, taking as the model of the Church of all times the original community of Jerusalem, which "remained faithful to the teaching of the apostles" (Acts 2, 42), and indicating the elders as overseers of this faithfulness (Acts 20, 17-38).

It is not necessary to develop in this connection a detailed theory of the ecclesiastic Magisterium and its centralization in the Magisterium of Peter's successor, although it would be difficult to present the lines that run in this direction in the New Testament: on the one hand the concept of tradition and succession that is made increasingly clear and on the other hand the theology of Peter. It is evident that the fundamental value of the apostolic succession consists precisely in the authority to preserve the apostolic faith, and that the consequent magisterial authority essentially comprises also the duty to show concretely the moral necessity of grace and specify it in the different periods.

With this the circle of our thought returns to the beginning again. The practice of faith belongs, in fact, to Christian faith. Orthodoxy without orthopraxis loses the essence of Christianity: the love that comes from grace. At the same time, however, it is admitted that Christian practice is nourished by Christian faith: by the grace that appeared in Christ and was attributed to the *sacramentum Ecclesiae*. The practice of faith depends on the truth of faith, in which man's truth is made visible through God's truth and is raised one step higher. It therefore radically contradicts a practice that seeks first to produce facts and through them establish the truth; against this complete manipulation of reality it defends God's creation. Man's fundamental values, which it gets to know from the example of Jesus Christ, are withdrawn by it from all manipulation. Defending the creation, it protects man. It is the irrevocable task of the successors of the apostles to keep the apostolic teaching present in this way. Since grace is in relation to the creation and the creator, the apostolic doctrine (as continuation of the teaching of the Old Testament) has to do with reason. Both flight into pure orthopraxis and the withdrawal of objective morality from the field of faith (and the Magisterium belonging to the faith) are equivalent, despite first appearances, to an accusation of heresy made against reason. In the one case reason is denied the capacity of knowing truth, and renunciation of truth is raised to a method; in the other case, faith is excluded from the field of reason and the rational is not admitted as a possible content of the world of faith. Thereby either faith is declared non-rational or reason non-believing or both. At the same time, on the one hand reason is taken as being univocal with its own time, which is not the case, and on the other hand its testimonies tally to such an extent with the standards of the time that truth disappears in time and the rational differs according to time, so that when all is said and done we end up by accepting the pure dominion of practical reason. The faith of the Apostle, as is seen from Rom. 1 and 2, has a higher concept of reason. St. Paul is convinced that reason is capable of truth and that therefore the faith cannot be constructed outside the rules of reason, but finds its way of expressing itself by communicating with the reason of peoples, accepting and refusing. This means that both the process of assimilation and the process of negation and criticism must start from the fundamental decisions of faith and has its firm points of reference in the latter. Reason's capacity of truth means at the same time the objective constancy of truth, which agrees with the constancy of faith.

The task of the Magisterium of the Church in the moral field follows from what has been said. Faith comprises, as we have seen, fundamental objective decisions in the moral field. The task of the Magisterium is first and foremost to continue apostolic teaching and defend these fundamental principles should reason yield to time or capitulate before the omnipotence of practice. The value of these principles is that they correspond to the fundamental knowledge of human reason, purified, deepened and amplified in contact with the life of faith. The positive-critical dialogue with reason must, as has been said, be extended to all times. On the one hand it is never completely clear what is really reason and what is only apparently "rational"; on the other hand there exist at all times both phenomena, the apparently rational and the appearance of truth through reason. In the process of assimilating what is really rational and rejecting what only seems to be rational, the whole Church has to play a part. This process cannot be carried out in every detail by an isolated Magisterium, with oracular infallibility. The life and suffering of Christians who profess their faith in the midst of their times has just as important a part to play as the thinking and questioning of the learned, which would have a very hollow ring without the backing of Christian existence, which learns to discern spirits in the travail of everyday life. The whole Church's experience of faith, thinkers' researches and questionings, are two factors; the watchful observation, listening and decision of the Magisterium is the third. That correct doctrine is not exercised automatically but requires the "exhortation and reprimanding" of the responsible pastors of the Church, was experienced by the Church in the first century, and for that very reason she formed the office of those who, with prayer and the laying on of hands, are called to the succession of the apostles. For the Church this office is indispensable today, too, and where her competence is challenged as regards essential decisions for or against an interpretation of morality following upon grace, the fundamental form of apostolic tradition itself is shaken.

EPISCOPAL CHARISMS AND PERSONAL CHARISMS

by Professor Marie Joseph Le Guillou, O.P.

MEMBER OF THE THEOLOGICAL COMMISSION

There is a great deal of talk in the Catholic Church today of the diversity and multiplicity of charisms, of their "liberation" or, more briefly, of a rediscovery of the Holy Spirit in the Church.

These expressions are certainly not false: they express a new fact which must be given a place in tradition even at the expense of giving rise to numerous ambiguities. To speak, in fact, of a charismatic Church in connection with the early Church may equally express a depreciation of the episcopal ministry and an awareness of a "charismatic" experience, and is thus to speak of the reciprocal interpenetration of sanctifying grace and the gifts given for the service of our brothers in the Church.

A glance at the history of the Church as a whole shows that several periods have followed one another.

There is a first period in which the abundant outflowing of charisms seems obvious. This appears particularly in Paul's epistles or in the charisms given to martyrs (vision of the sky opening, etc. . . .), as all the literature of the second and third centuries testifies. But it is no less evident that probably since the Montanist crisis, if the charisms have not ceased to continue in the Catholic Church, they have lost their missionary dimension and have taken their place mainly in the line of direct personal relations with God. This means, as Mulhen realized, that sanctifying grace and the institution of the ecclesial ministry had together practically absorbed the charismatic grace of evangelical services. What is now beginning to appear again is a restructuring along the lines of the great tradition of the Church. The experience of Trinitarian life in the mission of the Spirit is now seen to be integrated in the total offering of the person for the setting up of the Kingdom of God in brotherly service. The heart of everything is in fact charity. And it is a charity that must be shown forth in the spiritual gifts (1 Cor. 14, 1) which place the faithful in the service of the communion of saints. It can perhaps be said, but on condition that the ambiguities to which we will return are avoided, that the crisis that is shaking the Church today aims at a "liberation" of charisms in the service of the unity of the Church. We are certainly at the dawn of a new era in the history of the Church.

1. A Spiritual Community

That the Christian life is a life in the Spirit, or rather that "the Spirit is our life" (Gal. 5, 22-24), is obvious for St. Paul and for the apostles.

"When we brought the Good News to you, it came to you not only as words, but as power and as the Holy Spirit and as utter conviction. . . . You were led to become imitators of us, and of the Lord; and it was with the joy of the Holy Spirit that you took to the gospel, in spite of the great opposition all round you" (1 Thess. 1, 5-6).

Two experiences correspond to each other:

— the experience of the Apostle first of all. The power of affirmation, the fullness of conviction, which penetrate Paul's proclamation of the Gospel, the perfect constancy, the signs, the marvels and miracles that support it (2 Cor. 12, 12), spring from the Holy Spirit to establish Christ's testimony firmly (1 Cor. 1, 6).

— the experience of the faithful also. They accept God's Word and live it despite opposition in the joy of the Spirit.

Thus they imitate Paul and Christ in their lives.

The Spirit seals the word of the Apostle, and confirms it in the faithful.

"You are yourselves our letter (of recommendation), written in our hearts, that anybody can see and read, and it is plain that you are a letter from Christ, drawn up by us, and written not with ink but with the spirit of the living God, not on stone tablets but on the tablets of your living hearts (2 Cor. 3, 2-3).

Therefore, the only thing that matters is to let oneself be "guided by the Spirit" (Gal. 5, 16), and enter this mystery of the Spirit which is "love, joy, peace, patience, kindness, goodness, trustfulness, gentleness and self control" (Gal. 5, 22-24).

The Christian's personal experience, however, is not exempt from ambiguities, so it must be submitted to ecclesial discernment because it is in the Church, for the Church and by the Church that the Spirit is given.

"In the one Spirit we were all baptised . . . and one Spirit was given to us all to drink" (1 Cor. 12, 13; Eph. 2, 22).

This fundamental conviction governs Paul's attitude to this experience of charisms.

1. *CONFIDENCE IN THE ACTION OF THE SPIRIT*

Paul is not at all mistrustful with regard to the charismatic manifestations of the Spirit. As early as the year 51 he takes the Thessalonians to task for regarding the charisms with too much reserve. "Never try to suppress the Spirit or treat the gift of prophecy with contempt" (1 Th. 5, 19-20).

He recognizes, however, that it is necessary to take care to verify their authenticity: "test all things—hold fast to that which is good" (1 Th. 5, 21). His *a priori* benevolence comes from trust in God, who has bestowed on his faithful the gift of the Holy Spirit (1 Th. 4, 9) and teaches them deep down in their hearts to love their brothers (1 Th. 4, 9). Paul is even proud of the fullness of spiritual gifts, which makes the action of the Spirit present and tangible, as it were, in the communities he has founded. Does he not write to his community in Corinth which boasts of its charisms: "you are the seal of my apostolate in the Lord" (1 Cor. 9, 4) or again: "You are yourselves our letter, that anybody can see and read" (2 Cor. 3, 2).

There is no more visible proof of the authenticity of his ministry than this fullness of the gifts springing from the hearts of the faithful, where the Holy Spirit is acting. It is this fullness that justifies him before the Judaizers who contest his ministry and his doctrine of freedom as compared with the law.

Paul refers again to a similar experience in his epistle to the Galatians. He reminds them of their experience of divine favors (Gal. 3, 2-4). Certainly, Paul is concerned first and foremost about justification and the interior renewal of the hearts of his faithful. But he does this without ever separating them from their charismatic experience, since he speaks to them of him who lavishes the Spirit on them and carries out miracles among them (Probable allusion to the charismatic powers of curing the sick and casting out demons).

This ecclesial experience of the Spirit—that of a body with various gifts (1 Cor. 12, 4-30; Rom. 12, 6-7)—is for Paul the testimony that the economy of salvation is active in the world. It is a testimony of the Spirit who configures the faithful, from glory to glory, to Christ, God's image (2 Cor. 3, 18). It is, as it were, the guarantee of his apostolic ministry and freedom: "God is the one who has given us the qualifications to be the administrators of this new covenant, which is not a covenant of written letters but of the Spirit" (2 Cor. 3, 6).

So for Paul every member of the Church is informed and moved by the Spirit as every baptized person is taught by the Spirit (1 Th. 4, 79, cf. Heb. 8, 11 and Jer. 31; this teaching could be compared with 1 Jn. 2, 20 and 1 Jn. 6, 4).

2. *THE PRIMACY OF CHARITY*

In the manifestation of the Spirit, not everything has the same value, of course. So Paul points to the excellence of charity, the charism par excellence, the charism of all charisms. It is the way (1 Cor. 12, 21). It is the fundamental gift that alone justifies all other gifts (1 Cor. 12, 21). And this gift is poured into our hearts from above by the Holy Spirit who has been given to us (Rom. 5, 5).

Charity constitutes the being of the Christian so radically that without it one is nothing and without it the other charisms serve no purpose. It constructs the Christian (1 Cor. 13, 1-3) as well as the Church. Charity builds the Church (1 Cor. 8, 1; Ep. 4, 16). The judgment to be passed on charisms, therefore, will depend on the support they give to charity, which constructs the Church. This charity is founded on the faith, which operates out of love, the Spirit is active and leads the soul to the experience of the gifts of God.

Charity means, therefore, the primacy of the testimony of love of God. It is the mystery of the charity of the Father, the charity of the Son, and the transfiguration of the whole being by the Holy Spirit, the transfiguration of being and acting which unites man within and without with the image of Christ and constructs "the new man" in freedom and holiness.

All virtuous life is thus within the life of the Church. "What the spirit brings is . . . love, joy, peace, patience, kindness, goodness, trustfulness, gentleness and self-control" (Gal. 5, 22-24) or again "the kingdom of God does not mean eating or drinking this or that, it means righteousness and peace and joy brought by the Holy Spirit" (Rom. 14, 17-18). The Spirit that unites heaven and earth communicates to Christians the sentiments that were in Christ Jesus (Ph. 2, 1). It makes us live the life of the Risen Christ, who puts us beside the Father (Col. 3, 1f). It makes us inhabit this world in a "paschal way," not seeking our own good but that of others.

3. *ORDER OF CHARISMS*

This pre-eminence of charity governs the hierarchy of charisms which, though subordinate to it, are nevertheless indispensable auxiliaries for the common good (1 Cor. 12, 7) and for the building up of the Church (1 Cor. 14, 4-12, 17-26). The charisms must build the Church since the supreme value is the unity of the whole body which expresses the unity of Christ and expresses the mystery of the Trinity (1 Cor. 12, 4-6). The hierarchy of charisms is then clearly seen: charisms in the service of the Word of God, apostolate, prophecy, doctrine; charisms of miracles and cures; service of caring and ruling; gift of languages and interpretation (always mentioned last).

We will not dwell here on the different lists of charisms found in St. Paul (Rom. 12, 6-8; 1 Cor. 12, 4-11; 1 Cor. 12, 28-31; 1 Cor. 14, 6), all the more so in that they are not in complete agreement. What is certain is that for Paul three things are clear: ministries are charisms, gifts of God communicated for the good of all; that the ministries of the apostles, prophets and doctors head the list of the charisms given to the Church; and that these ministries are essentially ministries of the Word. But these ministries do not exhaust all the gifts that God has bestowed on his Church: there is still room for a multitude of gifts and functions for which the vocabulary remains very fluctuating.

It should be noted finally that St. Paul uses the word charism to designate grace in the most general sense of the word. It could be said that it is the grace of Christian experience, perceived as grace of knowledge and illumination, but always grace of existng and acting as members of the body. It is a question of living according to Catholic doctrine in, by and for the body of the Church. This is so true that in St. Paul charisms often designate functions as well as gifts of generosity or quality of heart (Rom. 12, 3). He invites every Christian to act according to the "standard of faith" that God has bestowed on him. It will be seen, however, that in the Pauline lists diversity is more and more clearly subordinated to the initiative of Christ. It is Christ who gives his body the ministries it needs for the service of unity.

Mention could be made of the primacy, in St. Paul, of spiritual judgment and of the apostle's judgment. He exalts prophecy at the expense of glossolalia. The former constructs and strengthens the Church. The latter does not construct the community since it is unable to nourish itself and to praise God. The spirit is abandoned to suffering and to emotion which permits its old pagan substratum to emerge again. It gives rise to a situation which makes the Church resemble a gathering of madmen (1 Cor. 14, 9-11). Paul felt keenly the danger of religious pathos and emotionalism. God, it is true, grasps Christians in their whole being and manifests himself on the plane where demoniac forces come into play, but this divine condescension must disappear and vanish in the pure light of God, charity (good sense, decency, respect for the other's person).

So Paul's doctrine is clear. If all Christians are responsible together for their life in the Spirit, if they have to discern the Spirit, as Paul says, it is no less true that their life is subordinate to the judgment and apostolic experience of the apostle, which are normative for it. The role of the apostle is of prime importance for it builds on the only real foundation: Christ—the crucified Christ.

St. Paul's teaching is close to the teaching of the Gospel: to prophesy, to cast out demons, to cure the sick are works of Christ. They testify to his mission, authenticate his word, but that remains ambiguous in Christian experience. One can be invested with divine power, even raise up the dead, and yet commit wickedness (Mt. 7, 21-29). The only criterion is, therefore, faithfulness to the will of God, loving obedience to God's commandments: "you will judge the tree by its fruits," in incessant confrontation with normative apostolic experience.

4. THE TRUTH OF LIFE

In the same way John in his struggle against gnosis gives us in his first epistle a lesson of spiritual discernment. It is important to discern true spiritual experience from its counterfeits, to test spirits. "It is not every spirit, my dear people, that you can trust; test them, to see if they come from God, there are many false prophets, now, in the world" (1 Jn. 4, 1). The criteria proposed by St. John can be reduced fundamentally to two interconnected criteria: baptismal faith and the commandment of brotherly love.

The criterion is teaching "given from the beginning" (1 Jn. 2, 7) on the occasion of Christian initiation. This alone guarantees the authenticity of communion with God. It is confession of Jesus Christ, Son of God, who came in the flesh (1 Jn. 4, 2; 2 Jn. 4, 7), who came by water and blood (1 Jn. 5, 6) and who teaches us to give our lives for our brothers (1 Jn. 3, 16). "His commandments are these: that we believe in the name of his Son Jesus Christ and that we love one another as he told us to. Whoever keeps his commandments lives in God and God lives in him. We know that he lives in us by the Spirit that he has given us" (1 Jn. 3, 22-24).

We find again here fundamentally the same criteria: the Christian is torn between the inspiration of God and the temptation of the devil: the world and God, Christ and the Antichrist. This hard, fierce struggle can be ended only with the help and discernment of the Spirit, in conformity with the norms of apostolic experience (1 Jn. 1, 1-4).

2. Episcopal Charisms

This evangelical experience has continued in the testimony of the whole Church. Irenaeus speaks to us of the "certain charism of truth" found in the bishops.

"We must listen to the presbyters in the Church: they are the successors of the apostles, as we have shown. And with the succession in the episcopate they have received the certain charism of truth according to the Father's pleasure" (Irenaeus A.H., IV, 26, 2).

The unexpected formula, according to the Father's pleasure, enables us to discern the true meaning of apostolic succession. The bishop is integrated by the divine gesture of election in the benevolent plan from which the whole economy of salvation proceeds in Jesus Christ. The Father marks the apostles and their successors and thus makes them participate in the confession of the Son, which becomes the vocation of the whole Church. The charism of truth which brings the bishops, by succession, into the apostolic service of the Father's eternal plan, reveals the specifically eschatological dimension of their ministry. As St. Ignatius says, "Jesus Christ our inseparable life, is the one who fulfills the Father's purpose, just as the bishops established to the ends of the earth are to fulfill the purpose of Jesus Christ" (Letter to the Ephesians 3, 2).

In the apostolic succession, through a ministerial succession unfolded in time, the bishops form one body ensuring an eschatological function: the custody of the trinitarian testimony for the salvation of the world. This ecclesial structure, as a whole, refers to the mystery of Christ, who does not speak of himself, but all of whose glory comes from the Father and returns to him (Jn. 17). It corresponds to the structure characteristic of Christian truth, which is trinitarian testimony. The question: "where do you come from?"; "from whom do you receive your authority?" plays such an essential role throughout the whole Gospel only because it governs the whole problem of truth in the relationship, explicitly affirmed, with the One who sends. The absolute source of all mission and the apostolate is, in the last analysis, the Father.

This means that the episcopal ministry has an essential role in the Church: to subordinate all experiences and charisms to the spiritual discernment of ecclesial charity. There is on the one hand the unity of faith in knowledge of the Son of God and the maturity of the adult, and, on the other hand, there is the scattering abroad, of false doctrines and the immaturity of children who lack inner stability (Ep. 4, 14).

The Church is incessantly caught up between dispersion and unity, immaturity and maturity, doctrinal and moral wavering and complete adherence to Christ. The role of the episcopal ministry is specifically to build up the Church in the sense that the ecclesial action of God through the Apostles and their successors builds the community of the Church by discerning charisms in order to make them serve the good of all.

The episcopal charism is, therefore, essentially a charism of discernment. It is a kind of radar which detects ambiguities and leads the Church along the straight line of the experience of Christ's mystery. This is done, of course, together with the whole Church and this charism given once and for all, as the Epistle to Timothy reports, must be renewed incessantly by personal experience. Bishops have to experience their ministry as a "ministry in the Spirit" in the service of the community of the whole Church.

3. The Teaching of Tradition

Tradition has been particularly sensitive to the criticism of charisms made by Paul and by Matthew. It has tended to dissociate grace and charism and to stress onesidely the theological virtues and the gifts of the Spirit far more than charisms. But it realized that charisms (apostolate, prophecy, teaching, gift of curing, gift of languages) are gifts that the Spirit distributes gratuitously in order that Christians may help one another to develop and to manifest the sanctifying grace that is in them.

St. Thomas in particular understood perfectly that the whole spiritual tradition of the invisible mission of the Spirit was manifested at the very heart of the Christian mystery since it is a question of an experimental knowledge of the divine persons (I pars. Q 43 A 3 ad/2um). But equally, he saw that this charity must aim at the construction of the Body of Christ and the development of spiritual gifts. He writes: "if there is an increase of grace where there are grounds for considering there is an invisible mission, it is above all to pass to some new act or to a new state of grace; for example, when one is raised to the grace of miracles, to that of prophecy, or when, out of fervor of charity, one reaches the point of exposing oneself to martyrdom, to renunciation of all one's goods, or to undertaking some difficult task" (I Pars. Q 43, a. 6 ad/2um).

If stress is laid on sanctifying grace, on personal sanctification—and this must always remain in the foreground—St. Thomas does not forget the charismatic and, so to speak, missionary dimension of God's grace. He was aware that the two ways of experiencing God's one grace cannot be separated. They penetrate and condition each other even if they have structures that are formally distinct. St. Thomas declares this in a very fine text:

"It is true, he recognizes, that we can know the Son by certain effects of grace—charisms—other than sanctifying grace. These other effects, however, are not sufficient to cause Him to live in us or to cause us to possess Him. The gift of working miracles is ordained to the sanctifying grace which it is a question of manifesting. It is the same for the gift of prophecy and any other gratuitous gift—charism. Thus in 1 Cor. 12, 7, St. Paul names this gratuitous gift "a manifestation of the Spirit." It is said, therefore, that the Holy Spirit was given to the apostles to work miracles, because sanctifying grace was given to them with the sign that manifested the Spirit—the charisms" (Q. 43, a. 3, ad 2um et ad 3um).

It is plain that in this way the Spirit causes the whole contingence of the human history of Christians gathered in Christ's Body to serve the purposes of the plan of salvation: the charism of prophecy is only the charism of discernment of God's will.

Far from being overwhelmed by charisms, the hierarchy must recognize this varied collection of God's wisdom and sort it out through the discernment of the Spirit, who is given to it in conformity with apostolic experience. There are, furthermore, two admirable texts which specify the attitude of the hierarchy in its relations with charisms and which confirm each other: one is the conciliar text in *Lumen Gentium* 12, which is, as it were, the charter of charismatic experience, and the other is the admirable address delivered by His Holiness Pope Paul VI on October 10, 1937.

First the conciliar text, a prophetic one.

"It is not only through the sacraments and Church ministries that the same Holy Spirit sanctifies and leads the People of God and enriches it with virtues. . . . He distributes special graces among the faithful of every rank. By these gifts He makes them fit and ready to undertake the various tasks or offices advantageous for the renewal and upbuilding of the Church. . . . These charismatic gifts, whether they be the most outstanding or the more simple and widely diffused, are to be received with thanksgiving and consolation, for they are exceedingly suitable and useful for the needs of the Church. Still, extraordinary gifts are not to be rashly sought after, nor are the fruits of apostolic labor to be presumptuously expected from them. In any case, judgment as to their genuineness and proper use belongs to those who preside over the Church, and to whose special competence it belongs, not indeed to extinguish the Spirit, but to test all things and hold fast to that which is good."

The Holy Father's text is as follows:

"We rejoice with you, dear friends, at the renewal of spiritual life that is manifested in the Church today, in different forms and in various environments. In this renewal some common notes appear: the taste for deep, personal and community prayer, a return to contemplation and stress laid upon praise of God, the desire to dedicate oneself completely to Christ, great response to the calls of the Holy Spirit, more assiduous recourse to Holy Scripture, a widespread sense of brotherly dedication, the desire to offer a contribution to the services of the Church. In all this we can recognize the mysterious and discreet work of the Spirit, who is the soul of the Church.

Spiritual life consists in the first place in the exercise of the virtues of faith, hope and charity. It has its foundation in the profession of faith. The latter has been entrusted to the Pastors of the Church to keep it intact and help it to expand in all the activities of the Christian community. The spiritual life of the faithful depends, therefore, on the active pastoral responsibility of every bishop in his own diocese. It is particularly opportune to recall this in the presence of these ferments of renewal that arouse so many hopes. On the other hand, even in the best experiences of renewal, tares can be mingled with the wheat. For this reason a work of discernment is indispensable. This work devolves on those to whom the Church has been entrusted. It is their task "not indeed to extinguish the Spirit, but to test all things and hold fast to that which is good." In this way the common good of the Church, to which the gifts of the Spirit are ordained, progresses."

These texts—like the whole of our exposition—show clearly that the whole charismatic and pneumatic dimension of the Church is regulated at its very root by the christological and apostolic form, as St. Irenaeus stressed.

"Christ summed up everything in himself, uniting man with the Spirit and causing the Spirit to inhabit man, becoming himself the head of the Spirit and giving the Spirit to be man's head: for it is by means of this Spirit that we see, hear and speak" (Irenaeus, *A.H.*, V, 20, 2).

"The apostles, sharing and distributing to believers the Holy Spirit they had received from the Lord, set up and founded this Church which is ours" (Irenaeus, *Dem. apost.* n. 41).

The apostolic tradition and the succession of the bishops indivisibly ensure the presence of the confession of the faith in the Spirit within the Church which lives because of the trinitarian mystery. At the heart of the Church, they are responsible for the authenticity and vitality of charisms.[1]

OBEDIENCE IN THE CHURCH

by Hans Urs Von Balthasar

MEMBER OF THE THEOLOGICAL COMMISSION

The difficulty, often the tragedy of the Catholic Church in the world at any time, but especially in the world of today, lies in the fact that she exists side by side with the other purely natural societies as a visible organized community of believers. She is therefore judged by outsiders according to the same sociological standards as they judge these other organisms. The result cannot but be a caricature of the Church, which, because of her inner, hidden nature, known only to the faithful, is quite different from a State or an association and can be rightly judged, even as regards her external appearance, only according to this hidden nature.

Before describing the Church as the People of God, the Constitution *Lumen Gentium* speaks of her as a mystery; and she is, just as much as the mystery of the Trinity, the Incarnation of the Word, the Son of God, salvation by means of his cross and his resurrection. She cannot be separated in any way from these fundamental mysteries of faith and is an essential aspect of them.

This is not recognized by all those who—often in good faith—claim to adhere to the mysteries of the Creed, while in fact their relationship with the Church is no different from their relationship with the State, of which they are part. It is, in fact, an even looser one, because the State has at its disposal means to compel them to carry out their social duties while the Church relies entirely on the spontaneous cooperation of her members. This cooperation, however, is significant and fruitful only when a member knows the significance, purpose, operation and laws of the organism to which he belongs. And this, of course, is not something that can be decided upon or changed according to the will of individual members.

Today there is a tendency to consider as true only what is fully comprehensible and, if possible, what can be done by the qualified person. This is the concept of truth of a technical age. It tends to an ever increasing extent to invade and try to regulate the spheres of natural social life, the family and all relations between men. It is not surprising that it does not hesitate when it turns to the Church and tries to change her into something understandable to the human mind, in order to be able to control her. Inevitably, also the understanding and exercise of ecclesial obedience is fully involved, because in this conception of the Church the individual will obey any command if and to the extent to which he considers it reasonable and useful, in accordance with his supposed understanding of the nature and task of the Church. So he holds in his own hand the yardstick of his obedience. In the last resort, he obeys an idea that he has himself formed and approved. But if the Church is primarily a mystery, then she cannot, of course, be considered in this way. Therefore obedience will also take on another structure in the Church. What structure?

I.

In the first place, the Christian—and what follows applies only to him—must remember that the Church exists only "in Christ." Paul calls her "his body," "his bride" (to the extent that she is "one flesh with him"), his "fullness," in which he is completed. Such descriptions of the close connection between Christ and the Church show, in the first place that it is just as impossible to represent Christ without the Church—which would be a mere abstraction—as it is to represent the Church without Christ. And it is a question of the concrete Church, in the form Christ planned and designed her during his life and founded her after his resurrection; and as she believed and lived as the concrete community of the New Testament; the Church that also composed the holy Scriptures of the New Covenant as the expression of her living faith. It is not a question, therefore, of a Church that starting out from a "historical Christ," we could plan anew today in accordance with what we take to be the expression of his Spirit, presumably without reference to the authority which one should obey in the Spirit of Christ.

Of the concrete Church, as she began to exist after Easter and Pentecost, it can be said that she wished to be completely obedient to her glorified Lord, to whom she bore witness as the Risen Christ and who had been at the same time the historical Jesus. This Jesus, who had now revealed himself to believers as Christ, the Saviour of the world, had himself lived a life of perfect and absolute obedience to his heavenly Father. According to a remarkable expression of the Epistle to the Hebrews (5, 8): "he, Son though he was, learned obedience from the things that he suffered"; that is, He was obliged to learn from personal experience how agonizing and difficult it was. If, therefore, at the end of his path of obedience, He gave back "his Spirit to the Father" when He died and then sent this same Spirit from the Father to the Church, it is only to be expected—owing to the close communion between him and the Church—that this Spirit will be a spirit of obedience.

But just as Jesus was obedient to his Father in the Holy Spirit out of deep love—as can be seen from the word with which He addressed him "Abba," "Father"—so the whole Church is obedient to her Lord out of love. She owes him everything: her existence and with it all the individual graces of which she lives and which have been entrusted to her to administer for men and for the world. Loving gratitude is the heartfelt attitude of the Church before Christ and God. And it is just this attitude that is difficult for modern man. He thinks (he has been persuaded) that one who has duties of gratitude, clearly does not belong to himself, but is alienated from himself as a consequence. He has the source of his being outside himself, while to be really free, he would have to have it within himself. A strange idea in the light of the fact that every child is already (biologically) indebted to his parents. This fact shows in a deeper way that he does not have the origin of his person in himself, but (on the theological plane) owes it to the eternal Creator.

The Church is, therefore, in her totality the body of Christ which is perpetuated in history and which always remains indebted to its origin, never being able to break away from this origin. The individual Christian is never the whole Church, however. He lives in her as a member, a cell, a part of the whole. It must never be forgotten that the Church, as a whole, can be such only if she understands herself as united with Christ: by herself, without him, she would be nothing. Therefore the individual Christian shares, on the one hand, the outlook of the Church, of which he is a moment and, on the other hand, owes himself (his Christian being) not only to an independent Christ, but to the whole organism, Christ (head)—Church (body). He exists only to the extent that he exists as a part of a whole that transcends him, to which the Church belongs. He is a Christian in that he is baptized. But baptism is a sacrament administered and received in the Church and by the Church (by virtue of the authority and grace of Christ). He remains a Christian by receiving the Blessed Sacrament, which, more than any other sacrament, can be received only from the Christ-Church, and therefore the Christ-Church must be thanked. And it is the same for the other sacraments, and all the means of grace (of which the Bible is also a part), which are nothing but ways opened by Christ for the Church.

There is nothing to change, therefore, in the old affirmation of the Fathers of the Church, that it is impossible to have God (and Christ) as one's father, if one does not have ("before," they even say) the Church as one's mother. Nowadays many people think that this image of the mother, applied to the Church, is no longer a suitable one. But anyone who finds this image an unsuitable one, must nevertheless admit the truth of what it represents: that the Christian in his Christian being is indebted to the Church, the existence of which precedes his own, and not only as regards the beginning of his Christian being, but also for his remaining a Christian all his life long. If he is a real believer, then this knowledge for which he must be thankful will inspire in him, not the idea of alienation from self, but love; love for that which surrounds him, because it is greater than he is, but which has bestowed upon him, above all, deep awareness of himself, true identity and knowledge of the purpose of life. That is why St. Augustine addresses the Church as "my beloved mother, in whom the first fruits of my spirit are hidden" (*Conf.* 12, 23).

II.

At this point let us take a step backwards and ask ourselves what the freedom of an individual or a group within human society really is.

Our concept of duty and obedience will vary according to the answer we give to this question. We must, however, start from a mature conception of freedom, suited to adults, and not from an immature conception, such as a child might have. For the latter, the concept of "being free" coincides with that of "having freetime" with the holidays or a day free from school or getting out of school an hour earlier. Whether he likes school or not, it is a constraint, one of the many constraints laid upon the child's life so that he may receive the formation that human society considers desirable. But the child already has other concepts apart from the contrast between prison and freedom. A child is proud if he can accompany his father somewhere and carry his briefcase, or if he is allowed to help his mother to bake a cake. In this "being allowed" he feels promoted, he takes on importance. This is because he can participate in a world bigger than his own private world, a world the significance of which he understands only partly, although he has some idea of its general purport. A good education will aim at driving it home to the child as he grows up that he will find most satisfaction, will be most completely himself, when he carries out those functions in life that human society has reserved or entrusted to him. He who receives something entrusted to him, assumes also the corresponding responsibility. The weight of the thing laid upon him confers a new gravity on his inmost being. And in the experience of his own gravity there is also the experience of the deepest freedom.

Life, of course, will nevertheless remain divided into hours of work and hours of free time. In the first place, because every man physiologically needs rest to be able to work. And then also because, in modern society, the individual can be more and more easily replaced by others in many sectors of work. What was once a personal trade and profession, becomes a technical job today. The work of an apprentice or master, which had a certain individuality, is replaced by the mass production of anonymous "articles." A man placed in this activity can still tell himself that he is doing something useful, perhaps through attaining a record performance on the qualitative or quantitative plane. But it has become far more difficult for him to understand his contribution to the welfare of the human community as a personal one. Hence the tendency to interpret once more the concept of freedom, which in a real human society is strictly linked with that of responsibility, in a manner belonging more to the phase of childhood: the absence of an external coercion, being able to do what one wants. To make this shift clearer, let us take an extreme case: the great artist. For Mozart, freedom was equivalent to having time to compose, for Raphael, having time to paint: here profession coincides with vocation. Being able, being allowed, having to, are one thing; liberation and recreation are in creation. This is the model for the freedom of the mature man, who transfers emphasis from his personal activity to his life mission.

Such a person understands spontaneously that an authority and various functions of order are necessary in the State to guarantee the common good, that is, the best possible balance of the good of all individuals. He realizes at once that "being in authority" means primarily responsibility. And, because of this responsibility, corresponding capacity and possibility, specific delegated power and force, must be attributed to it. Nothing will be further from his mind than to consider this power an aggression against the freedom of the individual, repression (or restriction of the sphere of freedom) or frustration. Such concepts, applied without examination, correspond to the childish phase of the representation of freedom. In this phase every duty represents an external limitation on the sphere of my freedom, in which I "can do what I like." Freedom is interior, duty imposed is exterior. Anyone who views life in this way has not yet any experience of the meaning of vocation or becoming oneself by choosing the meaning of one's life.

Obedience in the Church is probably felt as being so heavy because most men, under the pressure of technical existence, have regressed from the mature to the childish concept of freedom. For this reason, to speak of "coming of age" in the Church is ambiguous. If there is a childish way of thinking behind this concept, "to be of age" means "knowing oneself what one has to do," not needing to receive indications from anyone else. To support this concept, people drag in the Holy Spirit and his charisms, personally distributed to every member of the Church. But Paul, who develops the doctrine of charisms, did not have any childish conception of freedom, but a mature one, the conception of one who is really "of age." A charism is the task assigned by God to individuals within the structure of the whole organism. As such it is primarily responsibility (for the whole), involvement (in the whole), fitting in with other tasks, just as in the body cells and limbs fit in with one another. The shape of every task is determined just as much from inside as from outside—by the adjoining tasks. In an organism there are no empty spaces between the various parts, in which each one can express its freedom.

Also in the Church a mature conception of freedom does not consider the task of guiding and the power of directing as an aggression. And here it is not even a question in the first place of whether this power of directing should be considered as bestowed by Christ with the keys or as (democratically) chosen by the "priestly" people of the Church. For where a really democratic spirit reigns, the elected authority is considered equally invested with the power to command as in other forms of government. Now, certainly, in the Church of Christ the directing offices were, without any possible (historical) doubt, instituted by him and endowed with the corresponding powers, and not, of course, just for the first generation, but for the Church as a whole, as she exists throughout the ages. To consider these offices as limitations "of the Christian's freedom" is childish, puerile. Not to do so, is a testimony of Christian maturity, which, in our technical age that has robbed so many men of the sense of their unique life mission, has admittedly become more rare and more difficult to attain.

III.

The Lord of the Church is Christ, who from his high position as the "Head," organizes the "body" and distributes both the permanent offices and personal charisms, as He pleases, for the good of the whole.

One of the tasks of the offices is to recognize charisms, reawaken them, discern them, and make them fruitful for the whole. And for this very reason one of the tasks of the charisms is to recognize the authority of the offices in the Church, to promote their rightful and smooth operation through behaving in an ecclesial way, instead of making it difficult with "Corinthian" conduct and provoking their severity, which would otherwise be unnecessary.

It is true that Paul knew already that office *as* office in the Church, which is made up of "holy sinners," is never popular, but will always be put "in the last place." It is humiliated and, in a certain sense, it must be humiliated (see Peter) but this is in no case a task for members of the Church. That office in the Church "must" be humiliated, is necessary in the same way as that "there must be separate factions among you" (1 Cor. 11, 19). Christians are not charged with producing separate factions, as for example to make pluralism more interesting in the Church.

It is necessary to be obedient to office in the Church to the same measure as the office has from Christ the power of commanding, giving instructions, establishing order, dispensing visible unity. The highest invisible unity is in Christ, and the highest visible unity is in the harmony of all his members. But the function of the offices of unity rising in a hierarchy, is precisely in the service of this harmony: the ministry of the priests, the bishops, and in their midst, at the top, that of the Pope. Obedience to this mission of unity is full if it is the expression of the will for harmony, and therefore obedience to the highest and express will of Christ. There are not two kinds of unity of the Church. Likewise, there are not two kinds of obedience: obedience to Christ and obedience to ecclesial office. While office in the Church works for concord, it is in the service of the development of charisms and is concerned about the true freedom of Christians, which is exactly the same as obedience to Christ. And since in freedom charisms obey Christ, they cannot rebel at the same time against the office of unity which He set up.

* * * *

All this free obedience in the Church is not carried out in fear and trembling, but in what Paul calls Parresia, sincerity, frankness, joyful trust. Ecclesial obedience has nothing servile about it. Christians are not fawning courtiers. Charisms and the office of government are, together—in one faith, one love, one hope—directed beyond themselves towards Christ, whom they obey lovingly, the office guiding and the charisms letting themselves be guided. There is an immediate relationship between Christ and charisms, which allows them, to a certain extent, to control whether the commands of the office are in conformity with Christ, and to contest it if it departs seriously from this conformity, in order to bring it back to the norm and direction taught by the Catholic faith. But where this deviation is not evident, the obedience of the charisms must aim not only directly at Christ, but also be real obedience to the office in the Church. Paul calls not only for obedience to Christ, but expressly to himself, as minister (e.g. 2 Cor. 10, 5 f). The ministry must also concern itself with the correct presentation and formulation of Catholic faith; everyone must recognize that it has here a grace for the discernment of spirits, and an overall view and knowledge of Catholic tradition. No one must claim—not even as a theologian—a better understanding of the faith as a whole. This does not prevent the office in the Church from considering the service of theologians with gratitude when they succeed in presenting the one revelation in a new, lively way, better suited to men, without taking away from its substance. Just here, both office and theology must together pay particular attention to the Holy Spirit, but in such a way that the office, esteeming and utilizing the contribution of theology, remains judge of its utility.

All the organs that serve as mediators between office and charisms—and Vatican II strengthened them and added new ones to them—have the purpose of avoiding any break in the People of God between a "commanding" and an "obeying" Church, any break between obedience to Christ and the Holy Spirit and obedience to the Church, and finally any break between harmony based on the personal responsibility of everyone and unity based on obedience to the ministry. This history of the Church is as a whole a proof that both aspects are interconnected and that with the loss of unity in the ministry, harmony in the faith is also lost. No real builder of inner harmony will oppose the office in the Church, as if its "exteriority" were a curb on inner freedom. The curb comes rather from all those who spread this mistrust; they sow discord much more deeply than they are willing to admit. For Christ's Church is one only: the holy Church is also the apostolic Church, and together they are the Catholic Church.

FREEDOM AND TRUTH

by Juan Alfaro, S.J.

PROFESSOR OF DOGMATIC THEOLOGY AT THE PONTIFICAL GREGORIAN UNIVERSITY, ROME. MEMBER OF THE THEOLOGICAL COMMISSION

1. We are going to discuss two fundamental dimensions of human existence, which, on the one hand, cannot be denied and, on the other hand, seem at first sight to exclude each other. Human freedom consists in the autonomous and creative power of choosing and deciding, which makes man a responsible being; the experience of his own responsibility is the concrete testimony of freedom. Truth, on the contrary, presents itself as something that imposes itself on the human spirit, as the evident presence of a reality which man has not created but which comes towards him with the light of its own manifestation. Are freedom and truth, then, two incommunicable areas of human existence? If they were, freedom would play no part in man's meeting with truth.

This thought enables us to realize that freedom and truth are two poles of tension in human life, and that the problem of their mutual relationship is, fundamentally, the problem of man's unity. Consequently the binomial freedom-truth has its place in any anthropology, philosophical or theological. It makes us face up to one question which is common to every man, believer and non-believer: what is man? It is a question that implicitly precedes faith itself, since its prior understanding is absolutely necessary for the understanding of faith. If faith is not the alienation of man but his fully authentic fulfillment, it must correspond to the structures of human existence. Christian life, and reflection about it, which is called theology *(fides quaerens intellectu),* will have to show that faith interprets in depth man's fundamental aspirations.

Paul Tillich has pointed out with remarkable intuition a distinctive feature of man, the most visible one, from which all analysis of human existence must start: man is a radical question of himself, that is, of the ultimate meaning of his own existence. It is a unique question: the question. Man cannot get rid of it because he lives it in consciousness of himself, that is, in the self-presence that sustains all his activity of thinking, feeling, deciding and operating. What am I? And above all, why do I exist? What is my future? This is the first and ultimate question, the first one in vital experience and the ultimate one in the order of definitive things, because all the particular questions that concern man point to and converge on it. It is the question that constitutes the human being; man cannot eliminate it without renouncing himself, that is, without ceasing to be faithful to the vital call that makes him a man. The question of the ultimate meaning of one's life is always there, *nel mezzo del cammin di nostra vita* (in the middle of the journey of our life), like the Sphinx before Oedipus. It is impossible to ignore it, if one wishes to live really as a man.

1. Meaning of Man's Existence

For this reason the question about the ultimate meaning of human life is not addressed exclusively to the sphere of thought and knowledge characteristic of intelligence, but inevitably affects man in the deep recesses of his freedom. Confronted with it man cannot split himself into subject and object, because it is a question of himself, of the meaning of his own life. Whether he realizes or not, whether he wants to or not, faced with this question the whole man is challenged and committed. This means that this question is indivisibly a problem and a task, and that consequently man cannot answer it except in a total act of understanding, deciding and operating, that is, in the totalizing act of his human condition.

Man can be defined as the quest for the ultimate meaning of his own existence. There is no definition of man more existential than this one: here lies the drama that constitutes human life. The radical quest of himself is an undertaking of the whole man. In it truth and freedom, far from excluding each other or from being merely juxtaposed, include each other at the deepest level of the spirit: freedom is immanent in truth, and vice-versa. St. Augustine realized this: "What does man love more than truth?" The quest for the ultimate meaning of his life demands of man the passion for truth. This radical attitude of human freedom constitutes man's deepest truth, that is, unlimited sincerity with himself, which implies the most demanding option of his freedom. To meet the truth it is necessary to open oneself to it, to have the courage to let oneself be illuminated by it.

The immanence of freedom and truth in man's answer to the question about the ultimate meaning of his own existence is of vital importance in philosophical anthropology, since it reveals the fundamental structure of man as "a being in project," that is, as called to carry out his own vital project. It shows that the answer to this question cannot be so self-evident as to exempt man from the decision of his freedom, and in this way it marks the dividing line between scientific knowledge and philosophical knowledge. At the same time it makes it possible to understand what man's situation really is when faced with the problem of God and in relation to Christian revelation. It is a situation that cannot be understood except in the light of the question that constitutes man, regarding the ultimate meaning of existence.

2. Man's radical question about himself implies the question about God and culminates in it; for this reason it is not possible to tackle the first question thoroughly without arriving at the second one.

Human existence has its constituent dimensions in man's relationship with the world, with other men, with himself and with history. Man is necessarily bound to the world in order to transform it with his thought and his work, and thus grow in his own being as a man. To the immense potential of world energy there corresponds the unlimited dynamism of the human spirit, which bears in itself the responsible mission of transforming the world. Man's essential link with the world includes the paradox of his dependency on the world and his transcendence over the world. In his action to transform the world, man finds himself up against the pre-existing reality of a world which he did not create and which is governed by rules not established by him. The world and its energy in a continual process of change are governed by a fundamental action which is not that of man but goes beyond that action and will always go beyond it. The world appears to man as the mystery of a permanent reality, prior to and independent of man, which is imposed on him and which he must accept as the tangible proof of his own finiteness. His action on the world is necessarily conditioned by the becoming of the world, the foundation of which transcends him absolutely.

On the other hand, man bears in the experience of his experience of his spirit an awareness of his own superiority over the world. Thanks to his capacity of reflecting about himself and controlling himself in freedom he can discover the laws of the world, foresee its course and thus dominate it.

These two aspects of man's relationship with the world converge in the definitive question about man and about the world: in their essential connection, are man and the world the mere result of a process of evolution immanent in the world, that is, of an impersonal dynamism without freedom? Furthermore, granting that man's existence presupposes the existence of the world with its energy and its laws, is man himself (who is distinguished from the world and is called to dominate it by virtue of the freedom of his spirit) the anonymous instrument of the immanent evolution of the world? To whom, in the last analysis, is man accountable in his task of transforming the world? To the impersonal dynamism of the world or to a personal being, who is consequently distinct from the world? Can man, in awareness of his personal being and his freedom, explain himself as the product of a destined force, a mere privileged moment of the impersonal process of cosmic evolution? In the analysis of man's relationship with the world there emerges man's radical question about himself, and finally the question arises of the transcendent personal foundation of the world and of man: God.

2. Question Raised by Death

Each man's connection with the world is inseparable from his interpersonal relationship with other men. All are united in the task of transforming the world and creating history. The interpersonal dimension of human existence projects a new light on the question about its ultimate meaning. Every man personifies for others an absolute ethical law of respect and love. The other stands before me as a value that I did not create, which is imposed on me and which I absolutely must accept; and for him I represent the same value, the same unconditioned law. It will never be licit to instrumentalize the other, deceive, oppress, kill, degrading him in this way to the level of the impersonal. The greatest sacrifice (even of one's own life) in recognition of the absolute value that the other has for me, just because he is a person, will always be ethically legitimate. What is the foundation of the other's absolute value for me, and of my own for him? The human community? But must not it, too, respect the value of each of its members? The foundation of the value of each man must be common to, and transcending one and all. And so? Must it not be the transcendent personal foundation, which we call God? In the question about the value of man as a person, we inevitably come up against the question about God.

In man's connection with the world and with the human community, there is included an event as extraordinary as it is decisive, in which the question about the ultimate meaning of human existence is posed with the realism of the visible and the tangible: the event of death. Man's existence in the world is doomed to be shattered completely. Death reduces life to a broken arc which, looking out upon the naked emptiness of nothingness, constitutes the most relentless question regarding existence in its totality. Death inexorably raises the question not only of the after life but of our life in the world here and now. It puts man before the clearest and inescapable vital dilemma: personal extinction in nothingness or personal survival, which, however, he is unable to obtain with any of the resources at his disposal in the world.

3. The Only Absolute Future

But if nothingness were the final stage in life, the whole of human existence would be finalized and sustained in its innermost depths by nothingness: the ultimate meaning of human life would be absolute negation, complete absurdity. Sartre had the sincerity to confess it: "It is absurd that we were born and it is absurd that we die." In this sentence there is an unquestionable truth: if death is a drop into nothingness, death is absurd, and therefore life, too, is absurd. But can man resign himself to dropping into nothingness? Would this resignation not be, fundamentally, the most serene and tormented despair? Faced with death (and consequently facing life) only two attitudes are possible. And they are as radical as they are radically different: to despair or to hope absolutely. The existential despair of man in his solitude, helpless by himself to cross the frontier of death, or hope that can have but one name: God. The radical question about the meaning of human existence cannot avoid the question about God.

The same break that death reveals in the existence of every man is seen in history as the work of the human community. The internal dialectics of history brings with it the absolute impossibility for humanity to give a definitive meaning to history. In fact, the indefinite future of every stage of history is the condition that makes history possible. For mankind to be able to carry out the task of transforming the world and creating history, it is absolutely necessary that there should always be ahead a future to construct in the world. A definitive or immanent fullness of history is not only utopian, but also contradictory. The history of humanity, like the existence of every man, bears, therefore, the question mark of the inevitably incomplete, of what is necessarily lacking in an ultimate future; even more, the threat of complete disappearance. Also the question about the ultimate meaning of the existence of the whole of mankind leads, in the end, to the question about God as the only absolute future of history.

If the analysis of the fundamental aspects of human existence shows that the question about its ultimate meaning necessarily culminates in the question about God, the conclusion must be drawn that also the answer to the latter question will have to be a complete act of man, an indivisible act of knowing and choosing. Freedom and truth reach their deepest reciprocal immanence here. Before the question about God man finds himself confronted, whether he wants to or not, with the necessity of a total "yes" or "no." To say that God exists is to accept him, and to deny it is to refuse him. Man debars himself in advance from all possibility of meeting God, if he is not ready to worship him.

3. Consequently, man's situation confronted with the question about God prefigures the specific structure of faith. The word "God" signifies the transcendent personal foundation of the world and of man, of his responsible action and his hope, and of the absolute future of history. The affirmation of God cannot but include the option of submission and trusting surrender.

Actually, biblical faith, both that of the Old Testament and Christian faith, implies inseparably united, an acceptance of truth (affirmation of the content of faith) and an option of freedom (confidence-obedience before God's word). Any reduction of faith to either its aspect of knowledge or to its dimension of trust is an equally arbitrary mutilation of biblical faith.

The First Vatican Council stressed the presence of understanding and deciding (freedom and truth) in the act of faith (DZ-Sch. 3008). The Second Vatican Council adopted and completed this definition, emphasizing expressly in faith the character of man's complete surrender to God (Constitution on Revelation, n. 5). But as early as the 13th century the theology of St. Thomas had obtained a deeper view of the vital unity between the aspect of freedom and the aspect of truth in the act of faith. The assent of intelligence and the choice of freedom are only two aspects of the same act, the act of believing. Between them there is a mutual priority and immanence. Understanding illuminates choice, the dynamism of which in its turn informs understanding.

Considered from the anthropological point of view, the act of faith includes a moment of freedom, because in faith man gives his own existence a new and definitive meaning, centering it in the mystery of God's self-donation in Christ. It also includes a moment of truth, because this choice would be an alienating illusion without knowledge of the motives that justify it as a really human decision. The certainty of faith—at the same time absolute and free (a paradox already noted by J. H. Newman), cannot be explained except within the mutual immanence of freedom and truth, characteristic of man's answer to the radical question on the ultimate meaning of his own existence. The anthropological fact that man bears this question within himself, and the character of the answer it requires, with its inseparable elements of knowledge and decision, constitute the indispensable basis for the theological understanding of faith. Man's structure as quest of the ultimate meaning of his own existence saves the immanence of faith, that is, it is the point of vital insertion of faith in man. Without this fundamental dimension of the human being, faith would remain really extraneous to our life, as something merely superimposed upon it.

4. Far from suppressing man's radical question about himself (the question that constitutes the indispensable starting point of all philosophical reflection), faith necessarily implies it, since without that question it would cease to be a really human option, it would cease to be faith. And since, as the answer to this question, faith includes a dimension of knowledge (truth), it can reflect about itself and thus give rise to theology.

M. Heidegger wrote that the believer cannot ask himself the radical question characteristic of philosophy, without renouncing his condition as a believer. He can only behave "as if" he were asking, since he already possesses in faith the answer to this question, which, therefore, is nonsense for him. The "asking" characteristic of philosophy, and the "believing" characteristic of theology are two irreconcilable attitudes that exclude each other (*Einfuhrung in die Metaphysik,* 5-6). In its double dimension as choice and acceptance of a content given beforehand, faith is radically incapable, he says, of real philosophic thought. The option of faith makes it impossible for the believer to ask himself radically the question of the ultimate meaning of existence. And the assent of faith, based on God's word revealed in history, prevents the believer from getting to the bottom of the question of being and of truth.

It is not possible to answer this penetrating observation of Heidegger's except by going back to reflect on the immanence of freedom and truth in faith. A faith that did not spring from absolute sincerity with oneself and from deep love of truth, but rather from the influence of the environment or social conventionals, would be belief without faith. It would be a contradiction: faith without faith. The interior disposition to seek the truth is what distinguishes real faith from fanaticism and conventionalism: the radical conversion of heart. And this attitude permanently constitutes the soul of faith. The believer cannot remain faithful to his own faith except within the radical question "why do I believe" and "what do I believe" ("what do I believe" is itself part of "why do I believe"). Faith, therefore, is not only open to the radical question on the ultimate meaning of existence, but requires this question if it is to be authentic faith and to understand itself as such. The transcendental knowledge (awareness of the option-assent) and the categorial knowledge (motive of the option and content of the assent) implied in faith, bring with them all the demands of the ultimate question. Faith seeks radical comprehension of itself: it demands "understanding."

4. Radical Situation

Heidegger's claim seems to suppose that the question of the ultimate meaning of existence takes place exclusively on the plane of knowledge. But this is just what a philosophy of existence cannot admit. When it comes down to this radical question, man is already committed; he cannot dispose of himself, splitting himself up into a pure object of his own reflection. The neutral situation of a "pure reason" before the ultimate question on my existence and my destiny, is illusory. Consequently, the difference between the believer and the non-believer does not consist in one case, in a search for truth conditioned by the prejudice of the option of faith, and in the other case, a search without frontiers. It is rather a difference between an option of faith, an option that is open to faith, and an option of non-faith. The difference, therefore, is met with on the plane of total existence, and not in the partial dimension of knowledge.

849533